Bethink Rabbi Benjamin Schultz

By the same author:

A. Bernhard Henry Gotthelf, The First Reform Rabbi of Vicksburg, Mississippi, 2001, Privately printed.

B. The Jews of Vicksburg, Mississippi, 2007, printed and published by Xlibris.

Bethink Rabbi Benjamin Schultz

Julius Herscovici

Copyright © 2012 by Julius Herscovici.

Cover: Rabbi Benjamin Schultz.
　　　　Courtesy Institute of Southern Jewish Life, Jackson, Mississippi.

Library of Congress Control Number:	2011963256
ISBN: Hardcover	978-1-4691-4215-9
Softcover	978-1-4691-4214-2
Ebook	978-1-4691-4216-6

All rights reserved. No part of this book may be reproduced or transmitted in any form or by any means, electronic or mechanical, including photocopying, recording, or by any information storage and retrieval system, without permission in writing from the copyright owner.

This book was printed in the United States of America.

1. Iuliu Herscovici, S.
2. Jewish history - Mississippi - Clarksdale.
3. Southern Jewish history.
4. United States - anti-Communism - Jewish anti-Communism
5. Communism and Judaism.
6. Jews in public life.

To order additional copies of this book, contact:
Xlibris Corporation
1-888-795-4274
www.Xlibris.com
Orders@Xlibris.com
96935

CONTENTS

Excerpt 9
Information for the Reader 11
In Lieu of a Preface 13
Acknowledgments 17

Chapter One-Who Is Rabbi Benjamin Schultz? 19
Chapter Two-Obituaries 21
Chapter Three-The Unabridged Text of Three Articles 32
Chapter Four-Letters from the Readers 43
Chapter Five-Communist Response 56
Chapter Six-Personal Recollections 60
Chapter Seven-Last Sermon 65

Index 75

I dedicate this book to the Jewish community of Clarksdale, Mississippi, who had the courage to stand up to the pressure of some Reform rabbis who opposed the hiring of Rabbi Schultz.

Courage is not the lack of fear, but the commitment to do what is right.

Iuliu "Julius" Herscovici
Vicksburg, Mississippi
August 22, 2011

EXCERPT

In Clarksdale, Mississippi, after the assassination of Martin Luther King Jr., a memorial service was organized.
Reprint with the approval of Mr. Curtis Wilkie

Clarksdale groped for an appropriate response. After discussions between Andy Carr[1] and Aaron [Henry],[2] a Sunday-afternoon biracial memorial service at City Auditorium was agreed upon. Only one man objected openly to the idea. The mayor, Kat Kincade, ordered the doors to the auditorium locked in an attempt to prevent the service. But Andy obtained keys from another source, and at the appointed hour, the auditorium filled to its capacity with an integrated audience of nearly two thousand people. Whites sat beside blacks for the interdenominational service. A choir from all-black Coahoma Junior College sang. Several ministers spoke and offered prayers. Presiding over the event was Rabbi Schultz, turned from his anticommunist endeavors to racial reconciliation (*Dixie* by Curtis Wilkie).

[1.] Andy Carr and his brother Oscar Carr were planters and businessmen. Both brothers graduated from Anapolis Naval Academy and served as naval officers in the navy. After they retired from the navy, they worked for civil rights in Clarksdale. Of the two brothers, Andy was more active in the political arena of civil rights.

[2.] Henry Aaron (1922-1997) was a pharmacist by training and owned a pharmacy in Clarksdale, Mississippi. He was the president of Mississippi NAACP.

INFORMATION FOR THE READER

This book was not written for personal financial gain or any other commercial reason. The royalties of this book will be donated to the Carnegie Public Library of Clarksdale, Mississippi.

Many copies of this book will be sent free of charge to public and academic libraries in the state of Mississippi, in the United States, and in foreign countries. In the state of Mississippi, among the public libraries selected to receive the book is Carnegie Public Library of Clarksdale, Vicksburg-Warren County Public Library, and Mississippi Historical Archives. In the United States, the Library of Congress in Washington, DC; the New York Public Library on Forty-second Street; the Hebrew Union College-Jewish Institute of Religion of Cincinnati, Ohio, and New York will be also receiving a copy of this book.

The Hebrew University of Jerusalem and the British Museum of London, England, are the two libraries overseas I chose to be given a copy of this book.

Iuliu "Julius" Herscovici
Vicksburg, Mississippi
August 22, 2011

IN LIEU OF A PREFACE

In the book *Toward a Meaningful Life* by Simon Jacobson, I found the following story:

> On a sweltering summer day, an old man went down into a cool cellar for some relief. The moment he entered, he was blinded by the darkness. "Don't worry," said another man in the cellar, "it is natural that when you go from light to darkness, you're unable to see. But soon enough, your eyes will grow accustomed to it, and you hardly notice that it is dark." "My dear friend," replied the old man, turning to leave, "that is exactly what I am afraid of. Darkness is darkness, the danger is convincing yourself that it is light."[3]

This story encapsulates the struggle and legacy of Rabbi Benjamin Schultz. All his life, Rabbi Schultz was a strong critic of Communism. Even his foes, detractors, and a chorus of anti-Schultz people never questioned the sincerity of his position against Communism.

In the United States as well as in Europe, many intellectuals viewed the criticism of Communism and the Soviet Union as nonobjective and a biased intellectual exercise. In an era in which Communism was viewed in many of the intelligentsia quarters as a benign philosophy that could offer many positive solutions, Rabbi Schultz was an exception. Rabbi Benjamin Schultz arrived at his anticommunist convictions by researching the state of Soviet Jewry. He concluded that the Soviet law against anti-Semitism was a paper shell—good for propaganda outside the Soviet Union but not

---

[3.] Schneerson, Menachem Mendel, *Toward a Meaningful Life: The Wisdom of the Rebbe Menachem Mendel Schneerson*, adapted by Simon Jacobson (New York: William Morrow and Company, 1995), 278.

a protecting shield for the Jews living in the Soviet Union. The power of the law of anti-Semitism was null.

Rabbi Schultz was never a doctrinaire, an ideologue, or a philosopher; but his historical contribution in combating Communism is incontrovertible. All his life, Rabbi Schultz kept the searchlight shining on the real face of Communists: their activities, their methods, and their promoters. Rabbi Schultz was a pioneer in the struggle to free the Soviet Jews from the tight grasp of the Communist regime. The data on Soviet Jewry gathered by Rabbi Schultz set the foundation that at the end led to the freeing of Soviet Jews.

In October 1947, Rabbi Schultz published three articles about Communist infiltration in religious organizations. The effort to demolish the career and destroy the livelihood of Rabbi Schultz as a congregational Reform rabbi started after he published these three well-documented articles.

After reading these three articles, the modern reader will find out how many of Schultz's critics were and are unmoored from the original context. This is why I considered it absolutely essential that the integral text of these three articles should be a part of this memorial brochure.

As in the story told at the start of this preface, Rabbi Schultz was aware throughout his life of the danger that uninformed people would convince themselves that darkness is light and that Communism is benign. The names mentioned by Rabbi Schultz in his articles were good people, but with political naïveté. Because they're artless, many honest people did not see the darkness of the Communist ideology, the danger of Communist practices, the deceitfulness of Communist propaganda, and the shrewdness of their Communist activities.

American Jewry has a long and proven history of fighting Communist activities in the United States. After the Second World War, combating Communist infiltration and activities on American soil became a top priority for all Jewish organizations. The American Jewish Committee was by far the best positioned to protect American Jewry against any false accusations. Working with government agencies, the AJ Committee exhibited sagacity in presenting the facts of its cases and total discretion in its activities. To this day, this way of solving problems is the trademark of the AJ Committee. With personal connections, discretion, reliable information, sound judgment, and prestige achieved during years of activities, the AJ Committee has been successful in protecting Jewish interests. The Anti-Defamation League has been historically successful in using the courts to protect the American Jewish population from unfounded labels.

The American Jewish League Against Communism was formed in 1948 with the sole objective of fighting out Communist activities in the United States. This small new organization complemented the work of two other major Jewish national organizations. Rabbi Schultz was the executive director of the American Jewish League Against Communism. This new organization successfully took the Jewish anticommunist message to the middle class and the blue-collar segment of the non-Jewish American people. This segment of the American population was not reached by the activities of the AJ Committee or by the ADL. The message that the Jews, like the rest of Americans, are strongly opposed to Communism was conveyed by Rabbi Schultz to union halls, the American Legion, and many women's organizations.

In the fifties, the United States Army was preparing a contingent of new recruits to be deployed in Europe. In the process of training for their mission in Germany, the army found out that many of the new recruits held the opinion that the Communists are Jews. To dispel this erroneous belief, the army asked Rabbi Schultz to deliver lectures and convey the truth about Jews and their attitude toward Communism. The army, with all the means at its disposal, decided that Rabbi Schultz was best equipped to mold the beliefs of the new recruits.

It is Rabbi Schultz's historical achievement that he took the message of the Jewish anticommunist position to the American blue-collar people. Unfortunately, Rabbi Schultz never received credit for his role in reaching out to a large and important segment of the American population.

Rabbi Schultz was the first who rang the emergency bell about the true state of Soviet Jewry and existing anti-Semitism in the Soviet Union. The smoke-and-mirror Communist propaganda about the happy life of Jews in the Soviet Union was first cleared up by Rabbi Schultz. Many years later, the successful emigration of Soviet Jews was made possible in good part by the door first cracked open by Rabbi Schultz.

This brochure is a *hesped*, a belated eulogy, a very small tribute to a visionary rabbi and perhaps one of the most misunderstood American Reform rabbis of the twentieth century.[4]

Iuliu "Julius" Herscovici
Vicksburg, Mississippi

April 19, 2011/Nisan 15, 5771, the first day of Passover

[4.] *Hesped*: Hebrew word for "eulogy" or "memorial oration. Talmudic literature also contains funeral orations.

ACKNOWLEDGMENTS

Two outstanding New York institutions—the New York Public Library and the Center of Jewish History—deserve the main credit for helping me write this book. Without the professional help of the librarians of these two institutions, the writing of this book would have taken much more time to complete. Special thanks to Mr. John Favareau from the Yonkers Public Library.

The Carnegie Library of Clarksdale, Mississippi, made a major contribution to the content of this book. I am indebted for the help given by the reference librarians of this small-town library. Ms. Linda White of the local public library deserves my special gratitude for the information regarding the pictures salvaged by Mr. Kinchen H. "Buba" O'Keefe of Clarksdale, Mississippi. The help I received from Lawrence M. Magdovitz, Esq., of Clarksdale, Mississippi, was important for me to gauge the contribution made by Rabbi Benjamin Schultz to the Clarksdale community. Lawrence M. Magdovitz, Esq., was gracious to send the pictures showing the tombstones of Rabbi Schultz and his wife, Charlotte Elkind Schultz. It would be unfair not to mention the name of Paul Kossman, Esq., of Clarksdale, Mississippi, who worked hard to settle Jews from the Soviet Union in Mississippi. Paul Kossman also encouraged me in my research of Clarksdale's small Jewish community. I am thankful to Abe Isaacson's children for their permission to use their father's writings.

For his dedication and unselfish help with the editing of the text, I am indebted to Joe Diamond. Ms. Nicole Grossu checked the corrections and made many sound suggestions during the writing process. Ms. Rivka Schiller, with competence, translated some material from Jewish newspapers. Because Yiddish is no longer used so much by the Jewish population, a treasure of information lay unused by researchers and historians. The two articles translated from Yiddish give my book a special balanced presentation of Rabbi Benjamin Schultz.

CHAPTER ONE

Who Is Rabbi Benjamin Schultz?

Born: In Brooklyn, New York, on March 12, 1906
Died: In Clarksdale, Mississippi,[5] on April 22, 1978
Parents: Joseph and Rose (née Minskey) Schultz
Ordained: Jewish Institute of Religion in 1931
Married: Charlotte Elkind on June 6, 1944

Professional training: University of Rochester, New York
    1926: Delta Rho Prize in journalism
    1931: Rabbi and MHL at Jewish Institute of Religion

Employment:
    1928: Fellow Bellevue Social Service
    1928-1929: Student rabbi at Temple Emanu-El, Englewood, New Jersey
    1930-1931: Rabbi at Temple Emanuel, Kingston, New York
    1931-1935: Assistant rabbi at Avenue R Temple in Brooklyn
    1937-1938: He studied and traveled in Europe while on leaves of absence.
    1938-1939: Lectured widely in the United States

[5.] In the Jewish calendar, Benjamin Schultz was born on Adar 1, 5666. His death occurred on Nisan 15, 5738, the first day of Pesach/Passover.

1939-1947: Rabbi of Temple Emanu-El, Yonkers, New York
1948-1960: Executive director at American Jewish League against Communism
1960-1962: Rabbi at Beth Tefilloh, Brunswick, Georgia
1962-1978: Rabbi at Temple Beth Israel, Clarksdale, Mississippi

Membership:
President of Westchester Zionist Region (1939-1940)
Director of Yonkers Red Cross
Member of Yonkers Rotary Club
Central Conference of American Rabbis
Member of Youth Instruction Committee
Member of Religious Education Association
American Jewish Congress (1931-1933) (He was a member of the National Executive Committee.)
The New York Board of Jewish Ministers
The New York (Metropolitan) Association of Reform Rabbis
Brooklyn Joint Relief Committee (chairman of 1932)
Child Guidance Civic Committee
Jewish Institute of Religion Alumni Association
Member of B'nai B'rith

Authorship:
1931: *Universalism in the Midrash*
1932: *An Intimate God: Is He Possible?* (Brooklyn Tractate Series)
1933: *Jewish Education* (privately printed)
Contributing editor of the *Jewish Post*
Translator from Yiddish

CHAPTER TWO

Obituaries

I was told and had read that at his untimely death, more than one hundred newspapers across the country marked the death of Rabbi Benjamin Schultz with an announcement of his passing. Never was it my intention to print an anthology of all the obituaries printed at the death of Rabbi Schultz. Also, I did not have the money or the time to research and locate where and how many American newspapers printed the news about the passing of Rabbi Schultz. A few examples of obituaries printed in this book will give the reader a balanced sampling about the life and work of Rabbi Schultz.

Services held today for Rabbi Schultz
The <i>Clarksdale Press Register</i>, Mississippi
April 24, 1978

Rabbi Benjamin Schultz, who was rabbi of Temple Beth Israel for nearly 16 years, died Saturday morning at 9 o'clock at his residence, 1124 Rose Circle, at the age of 72. He had been ill for about five weeks, part of which time he spent as a patient at the Baptist Hospital in Memphis. He returned home the Tuesday before his death.

Services were held today at 2 p.m. at Temple Beth Israel, and burial was at Beth Israel Cemetery. Rabbi Harry Danziger of Temple Israel in Memphis officiated. McNeil Funeral Home was in charge.

Rabbi Schultz was born in Brooklyn, N.Y., and reared in Rochester, N.Y. He graduated from the University of Rochester with a B.A. degree and received his degree as a rabbi and Master of Hebrew Literature in 1931 from Hebrew Union College-Jewish Institute of Religion.

He was ordained as a rabbi in 1931 and served as an assistant rabbi in Brooklyn from 1931 to 1935, at which time he became assistant rabbi at Temple Emanuel in Yonkers, N.Y., here he remained until 1948.

He was appointed Executive Director of the American-Jewish League Against Communism in 1948 and held that position until 1960. During this time, he received formal recognition for his activities against Communism from both the American Legion and the Veterans of Foreign Wars. He published numerous anti-Communist articles, including a series in the Scripps-Howard newspapers.

Rabbi Schultz served as rabbi of the Temple in Brunswick, Ga., from 1960 to 1962, after which he came to Temple Beth Israel in Clarksdale. He was elected president of the Coahoma County Ministerial Association after his first year here.

An authority on both history and the current political scene, he traveled extensively in Europe during the summer and spoke German, Hebrew and Yiddish. In addition, he read French, Spanish and Italian. One of the results of these trips was an annual series of Adult Lectures given by the rabbi at Temple Beth Israel where he shared his experiences and knowledge.

Rabbi Schultz had served as president of the Clarksdale Rotary Club and was elected District Governor for the 1976-77 term. His district included clubs in the North Delta and the large Memphis Rotary Club.

He leaves his wife Charlotte Elkind Schultz; three brothers, Clement Schultz of Tampa, Fla., Morris Schultz of San Diego, Calif., and Robert Schultz of Bayside N.Y.; two sisters, Mrs. George Gottesman, of Brooklyn N.Y., and Mrs. Louis Mahr of Royal Palm Beach, Fla., and several nieces and nephews.

Rabbi eulogized
Editorial, the *Clarksdale Press Register*
Clarksdale, Mississippi
May 15, 1978

The late Rabbi Benjamin Schultz was the subject of a column by William A. Rusher which appeared recently in The Commercial Appeal. The columnist said Rabbi Schultz "deserved to be better known by the American people—and fondly remembered by them."

Rusher recalls that in 1946 Rabbi Schultz, while serving at Temple Emanu-El in Yonkers, "became publicly involved in the struggle with which his name will forever be associate; the battle against Communism."

According to the writer the late rabbi saw "with supreme clarity" what he calls "the evil nature of Communism." Then he adds that, "Ben Schultz embarked on his private crusade."

The columnist then writes as follows:

Three articles on Communist infiltration of religious groups Schultz wrote in 1947 for the New York World Telegram resulted in his condemnation by the New York Board of Rabbis and his departure from Temple Emanu-El. But Schultz stepped up his attacks, becoming one of the founders and the executive director of the American Jewish League Against Communism. His plump, vigorous figure was often to be seen at meetings of anti-Communist organizations in the New York area. If the occasion was a dinner, Rabbi Schultz more often than not pronounced the benediction.

"As controversy over domestic Communism ran its course, the scars of the old battles made it impossible for Schultz to continue his ministry in the Northeast. Uncomplainingly he moved to Mississippi, where his never-failing kindness and humor stood him in the usual good stead. In 1976 he served as a district governor of Rotary International."

And it was in Mississippi, on April 23, that he died at 72. "Count me o'er Earth's chosen heroes" James Russell Lowell wrote. "They were men who stood alone, while the foes they agonized for hurled the contumelious stone." All Americans owe a debt of gratitude for the foresight, the forthrightness and the stubborn courage of Rabbi Ben Schultz.

Rabbi Benjamin Schultz, Crusader against Communist Infiltration
by Morris Kaplan
New York Times, April 25, 1978

Rabbi Benjamin Schultz, the executive director of the American Jewish League Against Communism from 1948 until his demise in 1960, died Saturday of a stroke at his home in Clarksdale, Miss.

He was 72 years old and, since 1962, was the spiritual leader of Temple Beth Israel in Clarksdale. For two years, beginning in 1960, he had held the pulpit of a temple in Brunswick, Miss. [Correction: Brunswick is in Georgia.]

But it was the controversy that followed his 12 year ministry as a rabbi of Temple Emanu-El in Yonkers that brought him to public notice. Outspokenly critical of Soviet leaders and their "fellow travelers" in the United States, he fought those who, he said, tried to identify Jewishness with Communism.

Censured by Rabbi Board

His departure from Temple Emanu-El in November 1947 followed a resolution by the New York Board of Rabbis condemning him for three articles he has written for The New York World-Telegram on alleged Communist infiltration into religious groups.

He was accused of having used "the smear technique of the scandalmonger, a technique entirely inappropriate for a rabbi, an endeavor to bring into question the loyalty and Americanism of religious teachers whose record for sincerity and patriotism is unimpeachable."

Rabbi Schultz called on the National Conference of Christians and Jews to investigate supporters of Communism in churches and sought to "root the Communists and fellow-travelers out of government, education, churches and synagogues."

He also called for an examination of school textbooks and in 1949 told the House Committee on Un-American Activities that there was a Communist conspiracy to inflame religious and racial minorities against this country.

"Blacklist" Promulgated

In August 1950 he formed a special committee concerned with the broadcasting business, where a "blacklist" of radio and TV actors, writers, directors and other personnel appeared in a booklet called "Red Channels."

After Senator Joseph R. McCarthy's censure by the United States Senate for his tactics in investigating alleged Communist infiltration throughout the country, the league's supporters dwindled.

In Clarksdale, Rabbi Schultz remained a critic of Communism, but he had lost his national forum.

He became a district governor in 1976 of Rotary International and was president of the Coahoma Ministerial Association.

Rabbi Schultz was born in New York region in 1931 and served briefly as an assistant rabbi in Brooklyn.

Surviving are his wife, the former Charlotte Elkind of Yonkers; three brothers, Clement, Morris and Robert, and two sisters Mrs. George Gottesman and Mrs. Louis Mahr.

A funeral service was held yesterday at Beth Israel cemetery in Clarksdale.

In the Workers' Movement
What Is Being Said Now in the Workers' World
By Y. Fogel
New York, *Daily Yiddish Forward*
Tuesday, May 2, 1978
Translated by Ms. Rivka Schiller

We don't normally write from the Workers' side / perspective [i.e., in the column pertaining to the Workers' Movement] regarding rabbis or religious figures. That subject belongs to another column. But in this case, we are making an exception in conjunction with the death of Rabbi Benjamin Schultz, who died during the past few days at the age of 72.

Rabbi Schultz was the spokesperson and founder of the corporation known as the "American Jewish League against Communism." Aside from that, he was a personal friend of mine, someone whom I highly valued. Incidentally, we became very close during the time when the Communist International Order was liquidated.

Rabbi Schultz's achievements are very significant. He made a major contribution in uncovering the mask of certain Jewish liberals who wore Communist *Tzitzit* [phylacteries].[6] During the period when he functioned [in this capacity], there were unfortunately a number of Jewish liberals who worshiped Stalinist gods and crossed themselves before the red icon.

When Rabbi Schultz created the above league against Communism in 1950, the organization hired two Jewish union leaders, Louis Nelson, Manager of the Knitgoods Local 155, and Charles Kreindler, Manager of the Blousemakers Local 25. This fact alone clearly demonstrates how effective and worthwhile the league was, and is now, under the leadership of lawyer Roy M. Cohn.

Rabbi Schultz drew the greatest esteem for his sincerity, his deep devotion, and yes, for his great boldness / audacity. One had to have the courage to tear away pieces and yank out the mask from under the Jewish Muscovite puppets, who danced along with the Bolshevik tango. To much disappointment and disgrace, there were unfortunately such types of acrobats. And credit is due to Rabbi Schultz, for revealing the people's nakedness.

May his memory be honored!

*

Note: Rabbi Schultz was not a founder of the Jewish Leagues Against Communism. He was employed as an executive director and worked with JLAC from day one.

[6.] The *tzitzit* are no phylacteries. The *tzitzit* are specially knotted ritual fringes worn by observant Jewish males. The *tzitzit* are attached to the four corners of the *tallith* (Jewish prayer shawl).

Benjamin Schultz
by Harry K. Danziger
Central Conference of American Rabbis
June 26 to June 29, 1978, Toronto, Canada
Used by permission of Central Conference
of American Rabbis. ©1978 by CCAR Press.
All rights reserved.

Rabbi Benjamin Schultz was born in New York in 1906. After graduation from the University of Rochester, he was ordained at what was then the Jewish Institute of Religion in 1931. His first rabbinic position was that of Assistant rabbi and Director of Education at Temple Ahavath Shalom in Brooklyn, New York.

When he assumed the pulpit of Temple Emanu-El of Yonkers in 1935, a position he held for twelve years, he found there more than a rabbinic calling. The administrator of the congregation was Charlotte Elkind, and the two of them grew from a partnership in the life of the congregation to a life of partnership in marriage. Having come to know them only in recent years as neighbors, I saw vividly the closeness and mutual love and support that passed between them. In his last illness and hospital confinement, I saw Lottie give to her husband the cheer, hope and confidence that each of us as rabbis would wish to bring to those whom we visit in times of life crisis. It became apparent to me that she was, for him, a rabbi's rabbi.

The rabbinate of Benjamin Schultz included stormy years in the turbulence of the 1950s. He left the pulpit to assume the leadership of the American Jewish League Against Communism, and it was for his activities in that role that he was best known to many of his colleagues. Those days were well before my time, and I came to know a Benjamin Schultz in his latter years in a far different context.

He became rabbi of Temple Beth Israel in Clarksdale, Mississippi in 1962. At his death on Pesach morning of 1978, Benjamin Schultz was mourned by his congregants and his community with deep sorrow reflecting great affection. Serving as rabbi to a small community of Jews in Northwest Mississippi, he had brought to them the comfort and consolation that is part of the rabbinic calling. At his funeral, one by one, the families of his congregation sought to bring to his widow some measure of that which he and she had so often brought to them—a sense of support, a pushing aside of the loneliness and an attempt to share the burden. In church after church in Clarksdale, memorial prayers were offered to his memory on the day following his passing.

Benjamin Schultz was no stranger to the lecture platform nor to the organizational world. He served as district governor of Rotary and president of his county ministerial association. He wrote a weekly column for three years in a national Jewish periodical and was active in many organizations, both Jewish and general.

When Benjamin Schultz left organizational work to return to the pulpit, he wrote that his desire was to "return to preaching the word of God and re-enter the mainstream of Jewish life." As rabbi for two years of Temple Beth Tefilloh in Brunswick, Georgia, and then rabbi of Temple Beth Israel of Clarksdale for sixteen years until his death, he sought to fulfill that hope. The tributes, the respect and the grief of his congregants and community are testimony to what he did. As he was remembered on Pesach of 1978, it was not his national posture in the turbulence of the 1950s that was the hallmark of Benjamin Schultz, but the day-by-day and week-by-week service to and teaching of his congregation as their rabbi and their friend.

Rabbi Benjamin Schultz; anti-Communist proponent
The Herald Statesman, Yonkers, New York
Wednesday, April 26, 1978.

Rabbi Benjamin Schultz, 72, formerly executive director of the American Jewish League Against Communism and chief rabbi of Temple Emanu-El in Yonkers until 1948, died Saturday in Clarksdale, Miss.

Born March 12, 1906 in Brooklyn, Schultz was a leading proponent of Wisconsin Senator Joseph R. McCarthy's Communist smear campaign of the late-1940s and early-50s. His anti-communist activities and a series of articles written by Schultz and published in the New York World-Telegram ultimately resulted in his resignation "under pressure" by the Board of Trustees, from the Yonkers temple.

In the Congressional Record on May 20, 1955, the then-censored Senator of Wisconsin gave a testimony to Schultz, saying "for many years, he has been hurling with deadly accuracy and with impetuous force his spear into the flank and belly of this contraption of deceitfulness."

After his strident anti-communist articles appeared in print, Schultz was denounced by the New York Board of Rabbis "for using the smear technique entirely inappropriate for a rabbi." He earlier had called on the

National Conference of Christians and Jews to "root the Communists and fellow-travelers out of the government, education, churches and synagogues."

In 1950, he formed a committee whose duty was to publish a blacklist of radio and television actors, writers and directors. A major target of his writings and speeches was Rabbi Stephen Wise, founder of the Jewish Reform Movement, whom he called in his column in the National Jewish Post, "the chief rabbi of the Communists."

In 1960, Schultz returned to the rabbinate in Brunswick, Ga., and transferred to Clarksdale's Temple Beth Israel, two years later. Here he became the president of the Coahoma County Ministerial Association and president of Rotary Club. He was elected district governor of the Rotary International in 1976 and was honored along with his wife with the Paul Harris Fellowship by the organization.

A graduate of the University of Rochester and the Jewish Institute of Religion, Schultz earlier served as an assistant rabbi in Brooklyn.

He is survived by his wife, the former Charlotte Elkind, whom he married in Yonkers in 1944, three brothers, Clement, Morris, and Robert, and two sisters, Mrs. George Gottesman and Mrs. Louis Mahr.

Notes, comments, and corrections:

In the above obituary, the author wrote inaccurate information. Calling Rabbi Stephen Wise a founder of the Jewish Reform Movement is inaccurate. The Jewish American Reform Movement was founded in July 1873, and Rabbi Stephen S. Wise was born in March 17, 1874. The Jewish American Reform was formally established in Cincinnati, Ohio, and Rabbi Stephen S. Wise was born in Budapest, Hungary. It is too bad that the reporter who wrote the obituary did not check the facts. The superficiality in presenting this information perhaps explains the other two errors reported in the same obituary. Rabbi Schultz never called Rabbi Stephen Wise "the chief rabbi of the Communists." This expression was first used and coined by the *Daily Yiddish Forward*; and Rabbi Shultz reported to the readers of the *Jewish National Post*, where he, on a regular basis, wrote the *Weekly Digest of the Jewish Press*. This error in the obituary is perhaps due to a lack of research by the author of the obituary. Finally, Rabbi Schultz was never involved in the writing of any blacklist mentioned in the obituary.

Entrance at Jewish Cemetery of Clarksdale, Mississippi
Courtesy Laurence Magdovitz, Esq.

Rabbi Schultz and his wife Charlotte Tombstone in the
Jewish Cemetery of Clarksdale, Mississippi
Courtesy Laurence Magdovitz, Esq.

CHAPTER THREE

The Unabridged Text of Three Articles

Written by Rabbi Benjamin Schultz

Commies Invade the Churches
Pro-Russian Fronts Win Over Pawns
from Protestant Clerical Ranks
Printed in *New York World-Telegram*,
Tuesday, October 14, 1947

Editor's note:

Although Communist inroads into union, governmental, civic, and other groups have been widely exposed, a field almost entirely unexplored is the penetration of religion by the Communists. The Rev. Benjamin Schultz, rabbi of a Westchester congregation, has written three articles on the subject for the *New York World-Telegram*, covering the Protestant, Jewish, and Catholic faiths. Active in the Zionist movement and a columnist for the *National Jewish Post*, Rabbi Schultz in October, 1945, was feted by all three faiths for ten years' service to his temple and to his city. The first of his three articles follows:

Communists have a foothold in our churches. Many key Protestant and Jewish leaders are their dupes or willing pawns. Catholic-born labor leaders and glamorized celebrities use their "faith" to lure Catholics into helping Communism.

Thus, Rev. Eliot White, retired assistant rector of Grace Episcopal Church, became a member of the state committee of the Communist Party. The Rev. Claude Williams, Presbyterian director of the People's Institute for Applied Religion, forgot his overcoat; stunned friends found evidence of party membership in a pocket. Boston's Methodist Bishop Lewis O. Hartman in 1944 sponsored the twentieth-anniversary celebration for the Daily Worker.

Recently, Bishop Hartman and two associates made history.

Appeal for Eisler

The bishop opposed helping Greece and outlawing the Communist Party—both on the same day. The Rev. John Darr signed an appeal for Gerhart Eisler, convicted Communist agent, while attacking "interference" with Russia.

And the Rev. Richard Morford, a Presbyterian, was cited for contempt by congress. He refused to show the books of the National Council for American-Soviet Friendship, of which he's executive director. Its national chairman is the Rev. William Howard Melish, associate editor of Holy Trinity Church, Brooklyn, who writes for the Daily Worker and marches in the Communist Party's May Day parades.

Look inside Protestantism at this pro-Soviet network. (We'll discuss the Jews and Catholics later.)

Bishop Hartman claims seventeen Methodist Bishops and four thousand ministers and laymen in his Methodist Federation for Social Service. Its executive director is the Rev. Jack McMichael, who led the party line American Youth Congress. The Youth Congress liked the Hitler-Stalin pact, and when President Roosevelt didn't, booed him on the White House lawn.

Writes for Worker

Also active for "peace"—until Hitler attacked Russia—was Methodist Dr. Harry F. Ward, professor emeritus at Union Theological Seminary. Dr. Ward was Mr. McMichael's predecessor in the federation. In 1945, he spoke with Earl Browder at a Lenin memorial meeting; he writes for the Daily Worker, praising Marxism.

But let's get back to the Rev. Mr. Darr, Eisler's defender, who says "nothing in the constitution of the Communist Party" is subversive. He manages the United Christian Council for Democracy, which includes Bishop Hartman's Methodist Federation.

Another affiliate of his council is the Rev. William B. Spofford's Episcopal Church League for Industrial Democracy. Dr. Spofford, who edits The Witness, unofficial Episcopal journal, wrote recently: "Those who are anti-Communist... are aiding the cause of Fascism."

These are strands—just a few—in the network that would shock the country, if wholly revealed.

Most laymen and clergy are pro-American. Communists are in a tiny minority but a disciplined one. Their sympathizers are strategically placed, as editors, officials, orators; they're full of pep. And just as a minority captured Russia, just as a minority seized Germany, so this minority hopes to get the church.

Yugoslav Tour

It wants the churches so that "religion," opposing the Truman doctrine, the Marshal Plan, and everything Russia opposes, will help soften America for Soviet aggression.

"The Bolsheviks are prepared to play any card available at any time," the Library of Congress experts said recently. Chief expert was John Foster Dulles. The Witness' Dr. Spofford dislikes Mr. Dulles and wants his resignation as a leader in the Federal Council of Churches of Christ.

This Council is fighting Red infiltration. It represents 28 leading Protestant denominations. But it was never consulted when seven Protestant ministers, led by the Rev. Guy Emery Shipler, made a speedy tour of Yugoslavia and gave Tito a clean bill of health.

The trip cost Marshal Tito an estimated $14,000. On it went pro-Soviet Dr. Melish and Communist Claude Williams.

Thousands of innocent Protestants are totally unmoved by the Church Council's anti-Red fight. Meaning well, they cluster around Dr. Melish's Soviet-American Friendship Council from which Harold L. Ickes resigned. He called its stand on atomic-energy control Soviet-appeasing.

Rural Drive

The pro-Soviet council's Rev. Mr. Morford tells them to read the pro-Communist clip sheet. In Fact, edited by George Seldes, a leader of those White House "peace pickets" before Russia got invaded.

Clergymen like Mr. Spofford, Mr. Darr, Prof. Ward, Mr. McMichael, Mr. Williams, and the Unitarian Dr. Stephen H. Fritchman (ousted as editor of the Unitarian Christian Register for his party line editing) are no dupes. They're alert and won't be caught napping when the party somersaults. They somersault too.

However, dupes must be had. So a few years ago, Dr. Williams hired "sharecropper preachers" down South to take his "religion" to the farmers. It was revolutionary, so much so that his Institute got funds from the Sound View Foundation, Inc., which helps finance the Daily Worker, New Masses, and other Communist outfits.

Sponsors of this rural brainstorm included Dr. Ward, Mr. Spofford, Mr. McMitchel, and Kenneth Leslie, editor of The Protestant magazine.

The Communists have more luck with city folks. Take the clergy, for instance. Around the Leslie monthly, unsponsored by any church, cluster 7,000 naive persons called "associates." It's pseudo-liberal, anti-Catholic, pro-Soviet. The Communist Rev. Mr. Williams, is an editorial adviser.

Collect Big Sums

Hardly a clergyman named above has not been associated with it. It's been a consistent focus of Communist propaganda.

For awhile, The Protestant worked the "fighting anti-Semitism" racket, collecting huge sums from Jews. Then the overall Jewish Community Relations Advisory Council denounced it as "inimical to the interests of the Jewish Community in America."

Mr. Leslie's assistant at the time, the Rev. Ben Richardson, was ousted by his church in Harlem. A chaplain in the war, he was discharged from the Army "without honor."

These are the forces that make the noise, exert the pressure. They help disarm America—but demand a clear field for Stalin. Some of their dupes, clerical and lay, are shocked to find conservatives work with fascists. Rightly so. But why should "liberals" work with Communists?

Earl Browder was asked once if the party might change Karl Marx's doctrine that "Religion is the opiate of the people." In a frank mood, he replied, "We expect religion to be eliminated." William Z. Foster, present Communist chief, in his book "Toward Soviet-America," foresees an American dictatorship in which the YMCA and Masons will be "dissolved." So will the Knights of Columbus and the Rotary Clubs. And of course, the political parties.

Bellhops for Stalin

To face Communism, the Protestant Church needs first eyes that are open. Then action. Spotlight the Red minority. Follow wise liberal clergymen who, like the Rev. John Haynes Holmes, Dr. Reinhold Niebuhr, and the Rev. William C. Kernan, grimly fight Communist infiltration into Protestant denominations.

The Rev. Karl Chworowsky, pastor of the Flatbush Unitarian Church, has the answer. "I now bend over backward," he said once to escape participation in commie fronts.

"I am heartily tired of unwittingly playing bellhop for Joe Stalin."

Commie Invades the Churches
Red Crocodile Tears Ensnare Some Rabbis
Printed in *New York World-Telegram*,
Wednesday, October 15, 1947

Editor's note:

Although Communist inroads into union, government, civic, and other groups have been widely exposed, a field almost entirely unexplored is the penetration of religion by the Communists. The Rev. Benjamin Schultz, rabbi of a Westchester congregation, has written three articles on the subject for the World-Telegram, covering the Protestant, Jewish, and Catholic faiths. Active in the Zionist movement and a columnist for the National Jewish Post, Rabbi Schultz in October, 1945, was feted by all three faiths for ten years of service to his congregation and to his city. The second of his three articles follows.

Out of murdered Jews the Nazi made soap, and the Communist made propaganda. But the Reds don't care a hood about Palestine. They're there to snare the Jews.

William Z. Foster, head of the Communist Party, spearheaded this pseudo-Zionist campaign of the Reds at a Palestine protest meeting last year in the East Side's ghetto. The rally was sponsored by his party.

A co-speaker was Gedaliah Sandler, assistant secretary of the Jewish People's Fraternal Order. President of the order is Albert E. Kahn, whose job is to dream up and write about "conspiracies" against Russia. His publishers never mention his membership in the Communist Party.

The JPFO aims to utilize leading Jews and does snare some for the party.

Run Atheist Schools

Thus, Rabbi Stephen S. Wise, one of the leading rabbis in America and a noncommunist, lent his prestige to a rally of this Communist front on Jan. 23, 1946. Moreover, he declared that, "Not a select few founded the Soviet government. The people did." Two months later, the rabbi in a sermon called for giving Russia the atom bomb know-how. He defended Soviet expansion and blamed it on our "withholding the atomic bomb secret."

The Jewish People's Fraternal Order, actually a fraternal and propaganda arm of the Communist Party, runs atheistic schools for children throughout the country.

Yet the Jews of Los Angeles support it through their central Bureau of Jewish Education, and the order is officially a part of the Los Angeles Jewish Community Council. But tell the average Los Angeles Jew that he's supporting a Red front and you'll amaze him.

It's the old church story again. In the Protestant faith, as we showed yesterday, party-liners too often get what they want and pull the wool over the eyes of the ordinary, amiable churchgoer. It's the same in the Jewish fold.

Zionists Die in Siberia

Red Britain-baiting dupes many Jews now. Russia hails the Jews-to the Jews and the Arabs in-Arabic.

Yet thousands of Zionists are dying in Siberian labor camps. Zionism itself is a crime in Russia. Religious schools for minors are forbidden, so is the teaching of Hebrew. And there's mounting evidence of anti-Semitism.

But let the so-called American Jewish Labor council—headed by Communist Ben Gold—picket the British consulate here and a few more well-meaning Jews are drown into the vortex of Britain-baiting. This council, they fail to realize, is the labor front of the Jewish section of the Communist Party.

They're ruthless, the comrades. They don't hesitate to set Negroes against Jews. Last February, they set out to capture Local 22, International Ladies Garment Workers Union. The union leaders are Jews and anticommunists. (That's anti-Red David Dubinsky's outfit).

Racial Instigation

A Negro girl was hired by the Red opposition to spread the word among her friends that the union's Jewish officials discriminate against Negroes, charged Charles Zimmerman, Local 22 manager. The Communists lost the election. Afterward, the Jewish Morning Journal called their tactics "racial instigation."

Despite such tactics by the Reds, the orthodox congregation Oheb Zedek in East Pittsburgh last year gave $100 to the JPFO for "the noble work you are doing for the orphans across the sea." This "work" is not recognized by the United Jewish Appeal, the overall organized relief effort of the Jews of America. But it makes fine propaganda.

So does the new Jewish Council to Aid Russian Rehabilitation, which so far aided only Soviet propaganda. Its releases leave one impression: Russia is fine and dandy, inside and out.

This new council's executive director is Leonard Golditch, who was formerly with The Protestant magazine. This is the pro-communist journal, unsponsored by any faith, which successfully collected money from Jews "to fight anti-Semitism" until it was denounced last year by the overall Jewish Community Relations Advisory Council.

Bible and Marxism

Look to this pro-Soviet network that intertwines the faiths. The Protestant magazine board includes the Rev. Claude Williams, Communist Party member, and several Protestant fellow travelers. Another member was Joseph Brainin.

As Phineas Biron, Mr. Brainin runs a widely read syndicated column in the Anglo-Jewish press throughout America. His column is party line. As one example, it boosts the Young Communist League under its current name, American Youth for Democracy.

Mr. Brainin sponsors the School for Jewish Studies. This Communist-promoted school cleverly sandwiches a Bible class in between courses of Marxism. After it opened last year, the party's Morning Freiheit boosted it thus, "More than at any other time, the Jewish masses need Marxist training."

It's probably the only school in America with two ex-convicts on the board: Morris Schappes, who served a year in jail for perjury in the exposé of Communists on city colleges' faculties, and William Gailmor alias Margolis, who stole autos during a nervous breakdown and has lately been plugging the Soviet line on the radio.

Sponsors Listed

Nonetheless, an orthodox rabbi, Abraham Bick, is a director of the so-called School for Jewish Studies. On the staff of the Jewish Day, Rabbi Bick graces pro-communist meetings. In 1941, he linked Marx with the great Jewish prophets by writing, "Marxism's spirit is the spirit of prophetic ethics."

Another of the school's sponsors is Dr. Joshua Bloch, director of the Jewish Division of the New York Public Library. He once wrote anti-Catholic articles for The Protestant. One more sponsor is the aforementioned Ben Gold and still another is B. Z. Goldberg, a director of that new Russian Rehabilitation Council along with The Protestants' Mr. Golditch.

Mr. Goldberg's daily column in the Jewish Day, a Zionist paper, follow the Red party line. His June 6 column commented favorably on the success of the Communist-dominated Hungarian regime in killing off what Mr. Goldberg described as an "anti-Soviet, pro-American" plot.

The Day, respected Yiddish newspaper, is not Communist. It has some anticommunist writers. But Mr. Goldberg writes effectively. His editor, William Edlin, incidentally, has spoken on platforms with Albert Kahn, Communist head of JPFO, and P. Novick, editor of the Freiheit, Yiddish counterpart of the Daily Worker.

Cronbach an 'Innocent'

Caught in the Protestant-Freiheit-School for Jewish Studies net is such an innocent as Prof. Abraham Cronbach of Cincinnati's rabbinical seminary, the Hebrew Union College. Justly known as a saintly man, he nevertheless sponsors the School for Jewish Studies. Informed recently of its Communist function, Prof. Cronbach insisted on staying. His prestige is valuable.

Of America's five million Jews, less than one percent is Communistic. Others are liberals who've been sold on Stalin's "liberalism."

Dr. Wise, for instance, sincerely believes that liberals and Communists can work together against fascism, as certain Protestant bishops and ministers also believe. Thus believing, they lend their names to sinister groups.

But the vast majority of Jews are represented by the American Jewish Committee, Anti-Defamation League of B'nai B'rith, Jewish Labor Committee (not to be confused with the front labor council) and the Jewish Daily Forward, the largest Jewish newspaper in the world. They are dedicated to fighting Communist totalitarianism.

Exploit Jewish Grievances

Still, commies are expert propagandists. They get into strategic spots. Among the Christians, their slogans are "peace," "civil liberties," and "Soviet-American friendship." Among Jews, they exploit just Jewish grievances over Palestine and the myth of "No Anti-Semitism in Russia."

The Communists are working hard on Jews, Protestants, and Catholics to soften America for Soviet aggression.

It's time to drive them from the church. And from the temple too.

*

Commies Invade the Churches
Red Use Prominent Catholics as Bait to Lure Masses
Printed in New York World-Telegram,
Thursday, October 16, 1947

Editor's note:

Although Communist inroads into union, government, civic, and other groups have been widely exposed, a field almost entirely unexplored is the penetration of religion by the Communists. The Rev. Benjamin Schultz, rabbi of a congregation in Westchester, has written three articles on the subject for the *World-Telegram*, covering the Protestant, Jewish, and Catholic faiths. Active in the Zionist movement, Rabbi Schultz in October,

1945, was feted by all three faiths for ten years of service to his congregation and community. The last of his three articles follows:

With unmatched effrontery, the Communists are using prominent Catholics to lure the Catholic masses into Red projects. And they get away with it.

Indeed, so successful have they been that the Catholic church, a great world force against Communism, is genuinely worried.

That's why loyal Catholics backed an anticommunist Jew for president of the powerful CIO United Electrical, Radio, and Machine Workers. Harry Block, endorsed by the Association of Catholic Trade Unionists, lost, and Albert P. Fitzgerald, the Communists' candidate, won.

Candidate Block heads the drive against the Red controlled of UE. President Fitzgerald parades his Catholicism. This makes him an invaluable front for the Communist leadership of the third largest union in the CIO.

It was his right-hand man, Julius Emspack, UE's secretary-treasurer, whom Louis F. Budenz, former editor of the Daily Worker, exposed as the mysterious "Comrade Juniper" of the Communist Party's inner circle.

Thus Christians backed a Jew in what Pope Pius XII called a united front of the "overwhelming majority of mankind who still believe in God and pay homage to him."

They acted to oust a Catholic whose professed faith was used to lure union men into Communism.

There's another one who attends mass each Sunday. He's Michael J. Quill, boss of the CIO Transport Workers Union who has been identified as a member of the Communist Party by a string of ex-Reds.

He goes to church just to be seen there, according to the Ass. of Catholic Trade Unionists. On weekdays, he attacks Catholic church leaders. These leaders, on their part, warn Catholic workers, "Don't be beguiled by a brogue."

A perfect example of such beguilement was a dinner staged for the Committee of Catholics for Human Rights in November, 1945. Head of this group is a fellow-traveler, Hunter College professor Dr. Emmanuel Chapman.

As a featured speaker, he brought in J. Raymond Walsh, radio apologist for Stalin and Stalin's American Red stooges. Name a Red front, Mr. Walsh, a Catholic, is almost certain to be on it.

All Faiths Enmeshed

Prof. Chapman has lent his name to such Communist fronts as the Congress on Civil Rights, American Committee for Yugoslav Relief, Council for Pan American Democracy and League of American Writers.

And here again the Protestant magazine's pro-Red network enmeshed all faiths. Prof. Chapman joined its pet project, the National Committee to Combat Anti-Semitism; which was highly touted by the Daily Worker. The magazine itself kept up its anti-Catholic barrage. Evidently, Prof. Chapman didn't care.

Still, his high-sounding "Catholic Committee" has used the names of priests and nuns on its sponsorship list. It even used an archbishop's. As chairman of a committee of Catholics, he in turn has an especially strategic value to Communist fronts.

A graduate from Loyola, Prof. Chapman taught at Notre Dame and Fordham and is now on the Hunter College faculty. His brother, Abraham Chapman, is an editor of the Freiheit, the official Jewish Communist organ.

In Hollywood's publicity mill, the Comrades exploit Catholicism for a country-wide audience. Catholic Emmet Lavery is president of the Screen Writers Guild. He is not a Communist.

"As a professed Roman Catholic," wrote the Hollywood Reporter on Aug 8, 1946, "Lavery makes an ideal front man for the guild's Communists."

Pointing out he joined the Harry Bridges Defense Committee, one of the Red's top-fight fronts, the Reporter added, "Lavery was a member of the pro-Soviet Writers Congress and a speaker at the Communist-inspired Mobilization for Democracy. He has been an officer of the Hollywood Writers Mobilization and Hollywood Independent Citizens Committee of Arts, Sciences, and Professions."

'Both Favor Marxism'

"Both these groups have come out strongly in favor of the Marxian ideology which Lavery's Church is fighting."

Mr. Lavery praises the "Gospels of the Apostles and the Encyclicals of the Popes."

In a recent radio debate, California State Senator Jack B. Tenney said of Mr. Lavery, "He's hiding behind the Catholic Church, and so does Leo Gallagher, a registered Communist in the City of Los Angeles." On the same program, Mr. Lavery dismissed the alarm over the Communist threat. "I say it's spinach." He added, "It is not sedition to be a Communist."

Mr. Lavery represents a trend. Out on the coast, in key Detroit and in industries like transport, the merchant marine, radio, and telegraph—vital to America's defense—the commies had a tough nut to crack. Many workers are Catholics. How can they be controlled by Reds?

So a new party line was born. Faith is "private." Communism is "politics." So the Catholic faith should not interfere with politics, that is Communism.

Recently, the Catholic War Veterans got worried over "two-timing Catholics."

The CWV defines them as "All who publicly profess Catholicism under circumstances . . . which make such profession suspiciously beneficial to suspiciously anti-Christian and anti-American cause."

So it sent questions to some Catholic celebrities, queries like, "What is your pastor's name?" "What public position have you taken on the following—the present government of Poland, the trial of Archbishop Stepinac, the Vatican vs. Moscow?"

Some of the key persons queried were Philip M. Connelly, California CIO vice president and assistant to Harry Bridges, who belong to the national council of the American Peace Mobilization, which the Communists created to sabotage President Roosevelt's defense program.

George Addes, secretary-treasurer of the CIO United Auto Workers, "greeter" of the Daily Worker and Soviet Union.
Josephine Timms, who was secretary-treasurer of the American Communications Ass. and opposed "ganging up" on Russia.
Also, Emmanuel Chapman, Michael J. Quill, J. Raymond Walsh, and Emmet Lavery, all mentioned above.

Most Remain Silent

Most of them made no reply. Mr. Chapman called the queries "shameful."
Mr. Addes replied directly to the CWV, "The suffering of an individual as a result of such attacks is small compared to the sufferings of Christ."
An Encyclical of Pope Pius XII said, "Communism is intrinsically wrong, and no one who would save Christian civilization may collaborate with it in any manner whatsoever."
How then can Catholic workers be duped?
Well, why does a vocal minority of Protestants allow itself to be used by atheistic Communists or a bloc of Jews ignore rabbis' sufferings under Stalin and Zionists' imprisonment—to follow the party line?
Psychiatrists might solve that mystery. We know the vast majority of all religions are not Communists. But they must be awakened. A minority took over Russia and Germany. A minority could paralyze America and are working now toward that eventuality.
The Church is powerful instrumentality—to strengthen this country or to soften it
Let's root the Russia-first network out of all faiths!

CHAPTER FOUR

Letters from the Readers

To the *New York World-Telegram*

On Monday, October 20, 1947 (two letters)

Praise for Revelation by Rabbi Schultz
By Nathaniel M. Miakoff
Secretary-Treasurer, Dress and Waistmakers Union of Greater New York
Manhattan, New York

A public service has been performed by Rabbi Benjamin Schultz in his articles for the World-Telegram exposing the infiltration of Communists into religious bodies.

As one who has observed at first hand the destructive role of Communists in the labor movement, I know to what lengths they will go to gain their ends.

Very rarely is so clear and damning a picture drawn of the pernicious influence in the churches of Communists and their fellow travelers. The courage of Rabbi Schultz in sounding the alarm to Americans of all faiths is indeed heartening.

*

Exposing the Activities of Communists Here
By Mary Lee
Jackson Heights, New York

May I commend you on your constant vigilance in exposing the movements of Communists in the United States? I have followed the articles of your Mr. Woltman for some time, and more recently the series by Rabbi Schultz, who shocks one with his information regarding Communist movements in our churches.

I hope some day this outstanding service of your newspaper and these able writers will be properly recognized by the majority of our "indifferent" citizens.

Tuesday, October 21, 1947 (nine letters)

Communist Infiltration of Churches Denounced
By Patrick F. Scanan [partially legible], managing editor, *The Tablet*
Brooklyn, New York

We have read with great interest the series of articles by Rabbi Schultz on the infiltration of Communists, or those who follow the party line, into the various churches and synagogues.

With reference to those who claim to be Catholics . . . we believe Rabbi Schultz renders a public service in exposing the "two timers."

No religion is injured by bringing to public light those who do not follow its principles or who are in sympathy with the anti-God and anti-American movement.

Congratulations to rabbi Schultz and the World-Telegram for this series of excellent articles.

*

By Rebecca V. Mc. Nelty [illegible]
Bronx, New York

The duplicity of the Commies in setting up machinery to hoodwink responsible religious leaders, is farther proof of the detailed effort of the Red element to divide the United States citizenry.

The series by Rabbi Benjamin Schultz will be a great service to the country, if they awaken in our easy-going fellow Americans, the realization that the Communists are not to be taken lightly, for they strive in every way to wreck our government and spread discord.

Our Jewish neighbors should be proud of this splendid contribution by Rabbi Schultz, in the important task of alerting all Americans, regardless of race, creed or color to the constant vicious menace of Communism.

*

By Ms. Anne Marie Addy
Brooklyn, New York

I was greatly interested in the fine columns by Rabbi Benjamin Schultz, concerning the work of the Communists to undermine our churches, and mislead our religious leaders. He is to be congratulated as well as the World-Telegram, for this great public service and we hope his timely warnings to Catholics, Protestants, and Jews will not go unheeded.

*

By Mrs. Grace Mulligan
(no address provided)

Your recent articles by Messrs. Woltman and McDonald and Rabbi Schultz, exposing Communist activities have been both interesting and informative.

You are to be highly praised for arranging to have such articles brought to the attention of your readers. Thank you for your first-hand information so fairly presented.

*

By Mary Ryan
St. Albans, New York

Accept my thanks for the fine pieces written by Rabbi Benjamin Schultz, explaining how Communists try to mislead our ministers and disrupt our churches.

I marvel how he obtained all these impressive information, and was pleased to see it appear in my favorite afternoon paper.

Keep up your good work in calling our attention to the many sneaky moves of the Commies.

*

By V. Lee
Manhattan, New York

We were amazed at the temerity of Commies trying to take over the churches of the U. S. A. Rabbi Schultz certainly is on the ball to get together all that data. We also think your newspaper deserves great credit for having him write those stories for your readers.

These great stories must have burned up the comrades.

*

By Fred Ihda Jr.
Mountain Lakes, New Jersey

The World-Telegram in its fight against Communism can not be commended too highly for publishing the informative articles by Rabbi Benjamin Schultz. The influence of Communism in religion does not often appear in the secular press even though sincere religious publications have been denouncing dangerous infiltration for years.

The three articles exposing Communist dupes in Jewish, Protestant and Catholic groups will no doubt be attacked by those who seek the destruction of all religions, nevertheless, right-thinking, sincere Jews and Christians have been awakened. It is now up to the religious leaders to fight and if necessary expel these hypocrites from their ranks.

*

By Mrs. Walter Grosselfinger [partially illegible]
Manhasset, New York

Rabbi Schultz's series of articles were broad and enlightening. After reading these and Wm. Newton's articles, may I suggest the press assume the tremendous responsibility, which should be a privilege, of publishing millions of papers, brochures, leaflets, in as many languages as possible stating clearly and briefly:

(1) the basic ideas of Communism, (2) the basic ideals of Christian or American Democracy.

How can intelligent leaders who have enjoyed Americanism fall for any form so obviously inferior in ideology or scheme? They can't know what they do.

*

By G. Petrusello
St. Albans, New York

Thank God for brave men like Rabbi Schultz, who are not afraid to call a spade a spade, and to defend our great country.

His series of stories on Communism in churches was the most exasperating thing I have ever read. I would never have suspected them of such brazen nerve.

Rabbi Schultz has done a great service to us in writing about this dirty work of the Communists.

*

October 22, 1947 (three letters)

More Endorsement for Red Infiltration Expose
By Matthew F. Kennedy
Chairman New York State Catholic Affairs Committee,
K. of C. [Knights of Columbus]
Brooklyn, New York

On behalf of the more than 80,000 Knights of Columbus in our jurisdiction, I wish to compliment the World-Telegram for publishing the three articles by Rabbi Benjamin Schultz.

By exposing an almost entirely unexplored field, Rabbi Schultz has alerted Protestants, Jews and Catholics to the sacrilegious penetration of Red-Fascists into the field of religion.

May we have more Americans of the caliber of Rabbi Schultz.

*

By Ralph de Telegano [illegible]
Publicity Director, Joint Board,
Dress and Waistmakers' Union
Manhattan, New York

Rabbi Benjamin Schultz deserves the thanks of all thoughtful Americans for his fearless series on the infiltration by Communists of our major religious groups.

And the World-Telegram is to be commended for not bowing before the pressure of certain figures in our religious scene, heirs of Elmer Gantry. Hush-hush at this time plays directly into the hands of the Communizers who would use religion as a cloak, while destroying it.

*

By Mary Burgos
Jackson Heights, New York

May I congratulate the World-Telegram on the publication of the most interesting articles by Rabbi Schultz on Communists in our churches.
I followed his articles with interest and chagrin and have called them to the attention of my friends and neighbors.
Rabbi Schultz is to be lauded for his painstaking endeavors to collect his amazing information for the benefit of your readers. You too share in his success for publishing his fine articles.

Please continue to keep us informed on the many and varied activities of the Communist fifth column in our midst.

*

Note:

Besides the above three letters, on the same day, October 22, 1947, the *New York World-Telegram* printed the following information:

Catholic Vets Laud Rabbi Schultz

The New York County Chapter, Catholic War Veterans, has voted thanks to Rabbi Benjamin Schultz and the World-Telegram for their work in exposing Communism in a series of articles that appeared last week.

Rabbi Schultz has demonstrated he is an outstanding American and through his fearless articles has shown himself to be an asset to the members of this community and the country at large, the group said (page 4).

*

October 25, 1947 (one letter)

Adding to Applause for Rabbi Schultz
By Viva LeCompte
Hampstead, New York

May I add to the round of applause for Rabbi Benjamin Schultz and his courage? His series of three letters in your paper, October 14, 15, 16, should have two salutary results.

First, the people, generally, will become [illegible] to the subtle use of them and their best interests against themselves by the subversives groups in the country. Second, there should be a reawakened interest in the church of one's choice by those who have been too interested in material things for too long a time. There is nothing more likely to bring people back, to make them fight for their own, than the knowledge that someone else is badgering it.

These letters of Rabbi Schultz have been called to the attention of someone who wondered what he might do to reawaken some spiritual life in this country which owed its beginnings to the desire of people to be allowed to worship freely: he was deeply concerned about our apathy.

*

October 26, 1947

Under the headline Schultz's "Articles Praised by Legion," the following information was printed in the *World-Telegram*:

In a letter to the World-Telegram, James P. O'Neill, National Commander of the American Legion praised as "most timely and excellent done" the three articles by Rabbi Benjamin Schultz which were published two weeks ago by exposing Communist penetration into religion. "It is the opinion of our subversive activities specialist of the National Americanism Commission that the American public not only has been badly informed on this entire subject," he wrote, "but is entitled to know the facts as gathered and presented by some outstanding newspaper chain such as Scripps-Howard."

"Your organization is to be highly commended in starting such an exposure which only scratches the surface of the entire problem.

"As National Commander of the American Legion, I can assure you that public-spirited journalism of this type is most highly appreciated by our 3.000.000 membership. I say this to offset such artificially inspired 'smear' campaigns as may naturally be expected to result from such a series."

Commander O'Neill asked permission to reprint Rabbi Schultz's articles for distribution to Legion chaplains.

*

October 27, 1947 (one letter)

Rabbi Abram M. Granison Makes a Statement
By Rabbi Abram M. Granison, Jewish Institute of Religion
Manhattan, New York

In your article of Oct. 21 with reference to Rabbi Benjamin Schultz, he is quoted as having said "Mr. Charles Schnall (president of the congregation) told me that Rabbi Abram Granison, a field director of the Jewish Institute of Religion, of which Dr. Wise is president, had spoken to him about my articles."

The fact of the matter is that I have not been in touch, directly or indirectly, with Mr. Schnall or with any member of the Temple Emanu-El of Yonkers.

*

To the *Herald Statesman*
Yonkers, New York

Friday, October 24, 1947: Public Gives Its Opinion (two letters)

Rabbi's Assault on Communism Wins Praise from This Reader
By Bessie L. Nevins,
216 Voss Avenue
Editor, the Herald Statesman

I would like to add a word of praise for the three splendid articles on Communism, written by Rabbi Benjamin Schultz appearing in the World Telegram last week. He certainly pulled no punches in using names. I have heard him speak in Yonkers and his pen is as mighty as his voice. He certainly is a credit to his city and Country. What the world needs in these critical times is more people like Rabbi Schultz.

*

Attack on Rabbi Schultz Held "Disturbing"
By Horace M. Gray
85 Rockland Avenue
Editor, the Herald Statesman

It is astonishing and disturbing that a gentleman of the caliber and reputation of Rabbi Schultz must encounter such an antagonism from his own parishioners when his stands firm against Communist infiltration into the fundamental moral institutions of the United States.

Rabbi Schultz merits the respect of every red-blooded individual in this city. We know where he stands and why.

It seems to me that those who are so violent in their demands for his head owe the community an explanation.

The moral issue is clearly defined. There can be no straddling in this Country.

*

Monday, October 27, 1947 (one letter)

Temple Emanue-El Member Says:
Rabbi Has Right to Give Views.
By Walter T. Fuchs
7 Cedar Place
Editor, the Herald Statesman

    As a member of Temple Emanu-El, and as an American believing in the American way, I would like to discuss freedom of speech.
    Throughout the United States, cities and towns are greeting or awaiting the Freedom Train, which explains the American way to all—including the freedom of speech.
    Rabbi Benjamin Schultz, a militant civic worker, a man respected by all, was asked by the board of trustees of his temple to resign because he dared to denounce publicly Communism, the un-American way, which he feels is gradually finding a foothold in the religious field. He openly denounced Communism and those who lean towards it, in a series of nationally-printed newspaper articles.
    Freedom of speech is the right of all Americans. No American needs to be ashamed of his convictions if he believes he is right. Freedom of speech cannot have any limitations, except those provided by law.
    Does a person in private life have to have the approval of anyone to say what he thinks? Why, then, does a rabbi, whose outside activities are carried on as a plain American citizen, have to have his writing censored by anyone?

*

Tuesday, October 28, 1947 (one letter)

Public Gives Its Opinion
Sack Asserts Rabbi's "Facts Do Not Support His Charges"
By Isadora Sack
30 Berkeley Avenue
Member and Past President of Temple Emanu-El

Editor, the Herald Statesman

I did not want to enter the unfortunate controversy about Rabbi Schultz's articles charging that Communism has invaded the churches but the letters to the Editor in Friday's paper impel me to call attention to the facts. I suspect the writers of the letters did not read the articles themselves, but rather that they read the stories about them.

I will not dwell on the propriety of a Jewish rabbi leading a crusade to rid the Christians churches of a Communist invasion, if that has occurred. I rather think that is a task for the Christian clergy and laymen. However, I am concerned about the article implying that Communism has invaded the Jewish synagogue.

What does the article say? What are the "facts" that Rabbi Schultz challenges the world to deny? The only clergyman named in the articles a leader of American Jewry, the founder of the seminary in which Rabbi Schultz was ordained, Rabbi Stephen S. Wise.

The article states that Rabbi Wise attended a Palestine protest rally sponsored by an allegedly Communist organization. Does that prove or indicate that Communism has invaded the synagogue? If not, why name Rabbi Wise in such an article?

The article states that a congregation in Pittsburgh contributed through the same organization, $100 for support of orphans across the sea. Does that establish that Communism has invaded the synagogue?

A professor in the Rabbinical seminary who Rabbi Schultz says is "justly known as a saintly man" is "accused" of sponsoring a school for Jewish studies conducted by an allegedly Communist organization. Does that prove that Communism invaded the synagogue?

Nowhere does he show or even intimate amidst all the scurrilous intimations with which the article is replete, that any rabbi or teacher has preached any Communist doctrine in any synagogue.

If the Communists, to further their own nefarious ends, do choose to endorse a worthy movement, does it require all the rest of us to pump on the wrong side of the cause in order to prove our freedom from Communist influence?

May one not contribute to the relief of orphans merely because the contribution is solicited by Communists? May one not support a worthwhile cause merely because Communists endorse it? May not a rabbinical teacher teach religious subjects to any willing students, merely because the school is sponsored by allegedly Communist organization? What nonsense! We may as well say that the veterans should oppose the state bonus because the Communist party endorses it!

Yet these are the "facts"—and others even more remote from the issue—upon which the article is based, to establish what is probably the belief of many, that Communism has invaded the synagogue.

This is a malicious untruth for which not a shred of evidence is presented in the article; a canard which a rabbi should be the last person on earth to invent and circulate.

*

Notes and Comments:

Isidor Sack's irritation with the favorable response of the readers is noticeable. Disrespecting the readers, Sack is alleging that the readers did not read Rabbi Schultz's articles. Sack's first reaction is to divide the Jews and the Christians. "To rid Christian churches of a Communist invasion . . . is the task for the Christian clergy," not of a rabbi. In this letter, Sack braves the public opinion and tries to point out the incorrect position taken by Rabbi Schultz. In his letter, Sack is using inexcusable misinformation. First, Sack wrote that Rabbi Stephen S. Wise is the single clergyman mentioned by Rabbi Schultz in his articles. The truth is there are three other rabbis named. Rabbi Abraham Cronbach, Rabbi Abraham Bick, and Dr. Joshua Bloch are all mentioned by Rabbi Schultz in his article. This is the first example that shows that Isidor Sack was not well enough informed to write about Rabbi Schultz's articles.

In his letter, Sack plays down Rabbi Stephen S. Wise's participation at a public meeting of a Communist organization. First, Rabbi Stephen S. Wise did not attend the rally; he was an active participant and delivered a speech to this Communist gathering. The meeting was a rally called and organized by a Communist organization. The people were mobilized to participate by a Communist organization. Isidor Sack does not mention the name of the organization. The Jewish Fraternal Order was the organizer, and this organization was on the Department of Justice's list of subversive organizations.

In the school of Jewish study, religion was part of a larger and comprehensive program of Communist indoctrination. Many years ago, Rabbi Abraham Cronbach was fired from the position of pulpit rabbi because he gave a sermon favorable to the Bolshevik revolution in Russia.

Isidor Sack does not have any reasonable arguments to justify the firing of Rabbi Benjamin Schultz. It is pathetic to read such a letter, which justifies the destruction of the reputation and career of a rabbi.

Only after Rabbi Stephen Wise's death in 1949 was the Jewish Fraternal Order expelled from the American Jewish Congress. The reason for this measure taken by A. J. Congress was that the Jewish Fraternal Order was an active Communist organization.

CHAPTER FIVE

Communist Response

Woltman Finds a Rabbi
By Morris U. Schappes
Reprint from Yiddish *Freiheit*
Official newspaper of the United States Communist Party
Published October 18, 1947

As expected, the American Communist press went in high gear to criticize Rabbi Benjamin Schultz for the three articles published in the *World-Telegram*. For this brochure, I selected from the American Communist press only one such anti-Schultz article. Here is the integral reprint of the article written by Morris U. Schappes:

*

Among the afflictions that have burdened the Jews for centuries, one of the most loathsome has been the Jewish informer. There are Hebrew words for these creatures: MOSRIM, MALSHINIM, DELATORIM.[7] From biblical days to the present time, Jews have had informers, and they have dealt harshly with

---

[7.] *Mosrim*, means "hand over," "pass down." In the Talmud, the word has a positive meaning. In the Middle Ages, the word was used to refer to Jews who handed over Jews to the Christian authorities. *Malshinim*, meaning "slanders," is not found in the Talmud and is part of the blessing number thirteen in the nineteen of the classic daily service. *Delatorim* is an interesting word found in the Talmud and other early sources. It is the Greek *delator*, meaning "one who hurts, causes harm." These three

them. Talmudic law provided the death penalty for them. In the Middle Ages, this law was revived by the Spanish Jews. But the breed of informer has always thrived in the soil of reaction; the more terrible the reaction, the more active the informer. In the Warsaw and other ghettoes under Hitler occupation, the informer was made a Jewish policeman enforcing Nazi laws, and entrusted with the task of rounding up the Jews to be sent to the crematorium. The ghetto underground executed informers as a matter of life or death for the Jewish people.

Today in our country, with the Truman-Hoover "loyalty" decree establishing an inquisition into the thinking of millions of government employees, and with the American reaction pumping up steam for ever greater aggressions at home and aboard, the low craft of informing has fallen on palmy days. One of the nastiest informers has indeed been awarded a Pulitzer Prize. Throughout the democratic civilized world people laugh, not without bitterness, at this signal American treatment of the informer.

Woltman, however, has modestly decided not to do his work alone; he has become an entrepreneur of informers. It is reported that he suborns informers, trains them, and has them sign articles that add at least a variety of authors to the WORLD-TELEGRAM's monotonous series of exposes that expose little more that the fascist direction of the Howard chain of newspapers. As his latest addition, Woltman outdid himself. He found the last word in respectability. He hired a Rabbi.

Now you do not waste a Rabbi, when you do get one for such work, on the unprepared reading public. Therefore on October 10, 1947, Lee B. Wood, the Executive Editor (himself) of the World-Telegram sent out a letter to every minister, rabbi, and priest in New York metropolitan area, announcing that on October 14, 15 and 16, 1947, there would be a series of articles by this Rabbi on "the foothold which Communists have gained in our churches" and urging all Reverend Sire who received the letter to announce this series to their congregations. Advance proofs were also sent out to a select list to whet the appetite. The world waited.

Duly the articles appeared, soberly headlined: "Red Fronts Find Dupes in Protestant Pulpits," "Red Crocodiles Tears Ensnare Some Rabbis," "Reds Use Prominent Catholics as Bait to Lure Masses." A careful reading shows that there are no facts there that have already not appeared in the WORLD-TELEGRAM. One thing, however, is new the signature—the

---

words lend a learned cast to Jews who criticize other Jews. (The meanings of the three Hebrew words have been given by Rabbi David Kline of Massachusetts.)

malice, the libels, the misinformation, the viciousness, the phrasing, the style—these are all pure Woltman. But the signature, the all-important, ultra-respectable signature is that of Rabbi Benjamin Schultz, of Temple Emanuel in Yonkers, N.Y.

If you have never heard the name, mark it well now. Schultz has a career ahead of him, perhaps not as a rabbi, but a career nevertheless. I should like to see photographs of him promulgated throughout the land so that you could memorize the face, because it is a face that may one day accompany American fascist storm-troops down American streets and put the finger on Jews, or on anti-fascist workers, or on rabbis or ministers or priests who are against fascism.

Schultz once obtained the Delta Rhe prize in Journalism at the University of Rochester; now he wants to be the second to win a Pulitzer Prize as a MOSER. It is reported that Schultz has been angling for the post of rabbinical adviser to the Hearst press, but has failed thus far. Having made the World-Telegram grade, Schultz may still aspire to the Hearstian heights.

Schultz wants easy honors. He admirers the title of Doctor of Philosophy for instance, but he does not want to do the work to get it honestly. So he finds another way. If you consult the Yearbooks of the Central Conference of American Rabbis, you will find that Schultz had himself listed as a Ph.D. in the year books for 1938, 1939, 1940, 1941 and 1942. But for the Yearbook for 1943 and thereafter he has dropped his claim to the Ph.D.! He had been perpetrating a fraud on his colleagues in the rabbinate and he was compelled to discontinue the use of a Ph.D. title that he had never been granted. If, therefore, Schultz is currently on the Religious Education Committee of the C.C.A.R. that is something for the C.C.A.R. to reconsider.

A couple of years ago. Schultz become a columnist for the NATIONAL JEWISH POST of Indianapolis. His column became so notorious for its misinformation, slanders and misrepresentation that the editor received a score of letters written by some very prominent Jewish leaders too. Recently the column was dropped from the NATIONAL JEWISH POST.

Within the past year, Schultz acted as informer against a fellow-rabbi, and, using his connections with the Anti-Defamation League, forced this fellow-rabbi out of a Jewish educational institution. Then on July 19, 1947, Schultz published an article in THE NEW LEADER, which served as a sketch for his WORLD-TELEGRAM series. Having made THE NEW LEADER, he was ready for Woltman's stable of informers. In his series, he smears in traditional fashion all progressive Protestant, Jewish and Catholic organizations and many of their leaders. In the Jewish field, he fastens upon the Jewish People's Fraternal Order, the American Jewish Labor Council, the Jewish Council to Aid the Rehabilitation of Russia and particularly the School of Jewish Studies. These institutions need no defense, nor do any of the persons honored by Schultz's objurgations. But you should know the caliber of this informer.

For instance, he pick on one well-known radio commentator who is a sponsor of the School and summarily smears him as a man "who stole autos during a nervous breakdown, is "an ex-convict" and "has lately been plugging the Soviet line on the radio." I do not know whether there is a particle of truth in this malicious statement, and I will not demean myself by inquiring of the gentleman in question. But ASSUME that a man did have a nervous breakdown and did, while unnerved, violate the law and expiate his crime by serving a sentence. By all ethical standards, society now accepts the man as having paid a sufficient penalty. But along comes a World-Telegram snipe and taunts the man! What God does this Rabbi Schultz serve by this viciousness? Has he any more right to the honored title "Rabbi" than Coughlin has to the honored name "Father?"

Or consider Schultz's denunciation of the Methodist Rev. John Darr because he "signet an appeal for Gerhard Eisler, convicted Communist agent . . ." Eisler was convicted because he would NOT turn informer and provide the names of those who helped him while he was working for the German underground! And his wife, Hilda Eisler, a brave Polish Jewish young woman, was spending a year in Hitler's prisons while Schultz was taking over his pulpit in Yonkers in 1935. And now little anti-Semitic hoodlums taunt the Eislers in the streets of Queens and break their windows every week, while "Rabbi" Schultz pillories the occasional minister with enough fairness, courage, and Christianity in his make-up to object to the abortion of justice in the Eisler case.

Schultz claims to have been on the Youth Instruction Committee of the Union of American Hebrew Congregations. Pity the youth and pity the congregation subjected to the warped spirit of a man with so low a sense of human dignity that he is willing to drag into the sewers of the WORLD-TELEGRAM the names of honorable rabbis like Stephen S. Wise, Abraham Cronbach, Abraham Bick, and Joshua Bloch. The rabbi turn informer is an abomination. Informing should be hereafter Schultz's sole profession—and let all decent people beware of him.

CHAPTER SIX

Personal Recollections

By Lyle Brooks

11/17/2005

Remembrances of Rabbi Schultz

I started Hebrew School at Temple Emanuel in Yonkers in 1942. Rabbi Schultz was the rabbi then & I knew him till he left around 1950.
    Also I knew him as a kind, gentile, caring individual.
    He Bar Mitzvah me in 1948-49
    He left (I believe was asked to leave) around 1950 at least partially because of his political opinion especially concerning Communism.

Lyle

*

By Philip Aronson
Delray Beach, Florida[8]

Dear Mr. Herscovici,

After having served in the U.S. army, I was discharged after the conclusion of World War II, and promptly enrolled in New York University, thanks to the G.I. bill I attend classes in the evening and worked during the day for Schenley Industries in the Empire State Building at the same time, I became greatly involved in the activities of Temple Emanu-El of Yonkers, N.Y. particularly with the young people of the congregation.

Rabbi Benjamin Schultz, the spiritual leader at this time, greeted me with open arms and together we worked for many years for the betterment of the Temple family. We were greatly appreciated and earned the love and respect of everyone.

On the occasion of the first High Holiday, I was invited to conduct the young peoples' services in the Vestry Hall while the adults worshiped in the main sanctuary.

I reintroduced, some of the rituals abandoned by some reform synagogues and as a result some of the adults who [illegible] my service were so pleased with the changes I made, employed them in the regular Sabbath service.

Whenever we could, Rabbi Schultz and I visited a book store on South [illegible] Av. around the corner from Eliot Av. where Rabbi Schultz live, and also around the corner from Temple Emanu-El on Hamilton Av.

We all rejoice when Rabbi Schultz married his secretary, Charlotte Elkind.

One of the treasured moments of my tenure at the temple come about with a phone call from Rabbi Schultz inviting me to spend the forth coming Saturday evening with Charlotte and him.

Upon my arrival, I was informed that I would be participating in the marriage ceremony between my close friend, Mark Gross, who I grew up with, to a young lady, Joan Hoffman, who I had introduced to him. Her parents were very active in the Temple at that time and whose father was the editor of The Herald Statesman published in Yonkers and served Westchester County.

[8.] To protect privacy, the complete address is in the author's possession.

Happily, I celebrated Joan and Mark's 55th wedding anniversary this past summer in White Plains where he is well-known for his real Estates Holdings as well as for the large accounting office he operates.

After thirteen years Rabbi Benjamin Schultz and his lovely wife, Charlotte, left Yonkers to serve a congregation in Clarksdale, Miss., where they were loved and appreciated and they remained there until their deaths.

Strangely, Rabbi Schultz died the evening of the first Seder as did his father.

Sadly all of the people we both knew have entered eternity and in the course of over a half a century photos and documents have disappeared.

O how I wish I could be of more help to you.

Please accept my sincerest wishes for you to accomplish all that you have set out to do.

Most sincere

Phil Aronson

PS: I am grateful to Rabbi Schultz for encouraging me to walk the right path leading me to a wonderful fulfilling life, working with no less than 12 rabbis.

I retired after preparing 850 young people for the Bar & Bat Mitzvah while serving the congregation as Executive Director for more that 33 years enjoying the title E.D

[Education Director] Emeritus.

*

By Abe Isaacson
Clarksdale, Mississippi
February 1, 1982

Note:

Abe Isaacson was a member of the local congregation and for many years a shofar blower. Abe Isaacson wrote about the history of the Beth Israel

Congregation of Clarksdale. Here are two excerpts from Abe Isaacson's writings.

*

Probably the most famous Rabbi was the late Benjamin Schultz, a conservative man from New York City, who was on time the head of a committee to expose Communists in this country. He decided to come South and love its way of life. He settled in Clarksdale even though he could have a position in a larger city, but this where he wanted to spend the rest of his life. He bought two burial plots in our cemetery for himself and his wife. They had no children. When he died about four years ago, all the metropolitan papers in New York and Los Angeles wrote obituaries stating that the country lost a patriotic man who loved America with all his heart. Clarksdale will remember him for the work he did in Rotary Club and other organizations. His beloved wife still lives in our community. (*Clarksdale Press Register,* Letters to the Editor)

*

From *A History of Beth Israel Congregation As I Remember It*

The last Rabbi we had was Benjamin Schultz who came here from Georgia. In New York, he was famous as a chairman of the Jewish Anti-Communist league. He led our congregation for a period of fifteen years until his death in March 1978. After he died he was given an obituary by a columnist that appeared in 165 newspapers all over the country, acknowledging his greatness and his courage in Fighting Communism at personal danger. We buried him here in Clarksdale at Beth Israel Cemetery and so he will remain as one own forever. When future generation visit the cemetery, they will notice the large marble monument that marks his grave. (Page 8 from a typed history of the Jewish congregation of Clarksdale, Mississippi. No date when it was written.)

*

By Lawrence M. Magdovitz
Attorney and Counselor-at-Law
Clarksdale, Mississippi

December 28, 2010

Rabbi Benjamin Schultz and his wife, Lottie Schultz, arrived in Clarksdale, Mississippi in the 1960s where Rabbi Schultz became the Rabbi for Congregation Beth Israel and Lottie Schultz was his executive secretary.

Rabbi Schultz accepted the job in Clarksdale for several reasons but in my opinion the primary reason was that because of his work in the McCarthy era, most congregations and fellow Rabbis were not his backers.

Rabbi Schultz's patriotic America views made his well liked by the Christian community in Clarksdale during the 1960s. His good relationship with the Christian community helped the Jewish citizens of the area.

Rabbi Schultz in June 1972, married this writer and his Southern Baptist bride in the Temple in Clarksdale. Although Rabbi Schultz was liberal in some ways, he was extremely conservative on other issues . . . in my opinion

During Rabbi Schultz's tenure in Clarksdale, the Jewish citizens enjoyed a better relationship with the Christian community than prior to his arrival and since his death.

I have gone to the cemetery where I have taken photos of the final resting place of both the Rabbi and Lottie.

Hope that this letter finds you and your wife in good health

Sincerely.
Lawrence M. Magdovitz

Note:

This letter is the answer to the author's letter.

CHAPTER SEVEN

Last Sermon

Rabbi Shultz's Sermon Omits Any Reference to Controversy
The *Herald Statesman*, Yonkers, New York
Saturday, October 25, 1947

Rabbi Benjamin Schultz, central figure in a nationally discussed controversy over a series of articles he wrote on Communism in the churches, made no reference to the situation whatever when he preached last night before about 65 persons attending a regular Friday night service in Temple Emanu-El on Hamilton Avenue.

The Rabbi discussed the links of remembrance between the living and the dead and their significance in human affairs and progress.

Trustees of the Temple, who earlier in the week had voted unanimously to recommend ouster of Rabbi Schultz to a congregational meeting called for the next Monday night, suddenly decided early yesterday to "postpone indefinitely" any such congregational meeting. The trustees had voiced a belief the rabbi has devoted "too much time and energy to other than religious matters."

"Our dead want to be remembered," said Rabbi Schultz on his sermon, "but if we remember them they are not really dead. That is why we have tombstones and memorial prayers and perpetual care of graves."

"But it is not only the dead that want to be remembered. Unless the living are remembered by someone, they might as well be dead. The loneliest spot in the world is New York City where amidst the gaiety and the laughter, a man can be alone without friends and wish that he were dead."

"What is the binding tie? The binding tie is love. If we love our dead, they are not dead. If we love our living friends and our dear ones only then are they alive and only then are we alive. It is only in the presence of death that we can appreciate the important things in life."

*

Note:

In the Hebrew calendar, the Friday on which Rabbi Schultz delivered his last sermon was Heshvan 10, 5708. In the cycle of reading the Torah, for this particular Friday, he was required to read the *Parsha* (chapter) *Lech Lecha* (Genesis 12.1-17.27), and Isaiah (40.27-41.16) was the prophetic reading.

The topics death and remembrance do not have any direct correlation with text of the scripture dedicated to this particular week. The sermon was more a personal soul search made in a moment of high anxiety.

*

Comment:

Rabbi Schultz delivered dozens of speeches and sermons and wrote hundreds of columns. Out of all his writings, if I had to choose only one to read, I would choose his last sermon. There is so much human feeling and such a personal touch in his words; it makes his sermon a unique farewell address. In his remarks, Rabbi Schultz did not talk about his achievements but about his legacy. Perhaps at the time he delivered his last sermon, Rabbi Schultz had made up his mind that he would resign his position as a rabbi of the congregation. For a public persona, his legacy is the acknowledgment of his achievements.

As rabbi, Schultz gave Hebrew names to babies born to members of the congregation. He presided over confirmation ceremonies and blessed couples entering into holy matrimony. For the sick and the bereaved, Rabbi Schultz was a cane on whom his congregants leaned for support, understanding, and advice. As their spiritual leader, Rabbi Schultz offered his congregants not only a place in the congregation, but also the space to fulfill their spiritual needs. During his twelve-year tenure as a rabbi, the membership of his congregation increased dramatically. In his last sermon, Benjamin Schultz did not accuse, did not explain, and did not apologize. He knew that he was right—and history proved him right—in his anti-Communist stand. As a rabbi, he was fully aware that no human being can undo what has been done, that no one can change the past. Because he felt he was right, he had no intention of retreating from what he had written and what he had fought against.

On the diploma of each rabbi, including that of a Reform rabbi, are written the words, "*Yoreh, Yoreh*" (May he decide? He may decide.) "*Yadin, Yadin*" (May he judge? He may judge.) All Reform rabbis who actively orchestrated the anti-Schultz campaigns and actively participated in the effort to discredit Rabbi Schultz did not use sound judgment. To render a verdict does not necessarily mean that the verdict is correct. In battling Rabbi Schultz, *Yoreh, Yoreh* and *Yadin, Yadin* were ignored by the rabbis committed to destroying his legacy and achievements. The biggest sin of the Reform rabbis of New York at the time was that they shunned their responsibilities. Sixty-plus years after the events, it is hard for us to understand the loud chorus of hate and vengeance against Rabbi Schultz. Rabbi Shimon Bar-Yohai has left us this sentence, "This episode cannot be expressed in words, nor is it possible to comment on its implications."[9]

Like the biblical Joseph, Rabbi Schultz suffered at the hands of Jews. Yes, in our long history, we Jews have suffered many times from the actions and words of our fellow Jews. Rabbi Benjamin Schultz was one on whom much pain and injustice were inflicted by some Jews. The board of trustees of the Yonkers congregation rushed to genuflect before the demands of the board of the Reform rabbis of New York and decided to fire Rabbi Schultz. No questions asked. It was logical to ask the leadership of the congregation why the Central Conference of Reform Rabbis keeps Rabbi Schultz as a member while the congregation chose to fire him?[10] By their decision, the leadership of the Reform congregation of Yonkers volunteered to be the executioner for some radically activist rabbis.

A rabbi from a nearby congregation pointed out to the board that the firing of Rabbi Schultz could backfire on them. Afraid of the American legal system, the leadership of the congregation of Yonkers decided to reverse its decision. They announced they had indefinitely postponed Rabbi Schultz's

---

9. Quotation taken from Elie Weisel's *Messengers of God: Biblical Portraits and Legends* (Summit Books, 1976), 45.
10. Central Conference of Reform Rabbis (CCRR) is the reform rabbinic association founded in 1889 by Isaac Mayer Wise.

firing. It did not take long for the board of trustees to add cowardliness to its previous genuflection. The irresponsible behavior of the congregation's leadership was pathetic.

In our time, in our country, lived a legendary rabbi who found the courage to stand with and for the United States and the Jewish people. Despite the truth that he stood for, Shultz's enemies succeeded in demonizing him. The success of the anti-Schultz campaign is unsettling and is of great concern.

What remains of Rabbi Schultz? An example—one not to be forgotten.

Postscript

Early Evidence of Red Evil
by Morrie Ryskind
Memphis, the *Commercial Appeal*
February 28, 1971

I fear our Sovietphiles and I will never used understand each other. If I am astounded by their ignoring 50 years of Red double-dealing, they are equally puzzled by my distrust. Perhaps four recent items, seemingly unrelated, that combine to take me down Memory Lane, may explain more of "how I got that way."

Currently, even the liberal press—which usually is hard on "Red baiting"—has taken cognizance of Russia's "new" anti-Semitism; A. A. Berle, a noted adviser to FDR has just passed away in New York;[11] Rabbi Benjamin Schultz phoned me from Clarksdale, Miss., to make sure the Los Angeles earthquake had not harm us; and Isaac Don Levine, famed expert on Russia, now at his summer home in California, is due to have dinner with us this week.

WHAT TIES them together in my mind? Well, let's take the good rabbi first. When he was head of a temple in Yonkers, N.Y., he interviewed a number of Jews who had fled the Soviet paradise. Aroused by their revelations of the tragedies resulting from the Bolsheviks' calculated anti-Semitism, he

---

[11.] Adolf Augustus Berle Jr. (1895-1971)—lawyer, educator, author, and diplomat—was an important member of President F. D. Roosevelt's brain trust. He graduated from Harvard Law School at age twenty-one and became the youngest graduate in the school's history.

wrote an article which appeared in the Hearst newspapers in August, 1946. A sample excerpt:

"The 150.000 Jews who escaped into Russia from Nazi-occupied Poland were sent to heavy labor camps in Siberia. One third died within six years."

The findings were contrary to liberal gospel which regarded Communism as the wave of the future, and were denounced by some ministers—Jewish and Christians—as "witch hunts" designed to divide us from our brave ally. Good old Joe anti-Semitic? Rubbish!

RABBI SCHULTZ took a look at the record of the main denouncers—and found them not so kosher. And when he subsequently ran a series on the fellow travelers in church and synagogue, citing chapter and verse, all hell—or should I say heaven?—broke loose.

Later, in 1949, a Russian refugee who had been a member of the Moscow Soviet, Gregor Aronson, wrote a detailed account (in Yiddish) of the anti-Semitic measures he had seen enforced. Rabbi Schultz translated this and it was published by the American Jewish League Against Communism, of which he had become executive director. All of the material was later confirmed, but at the time the league was condemned as fascistic. (At the time incidentally, both Don Levine and I were on the board of directors.)[12]

When Wittaker Chambers decided to break with the Red conspiracy, he turned to Don Levine in the hope of getting the story of the cabal to the government. Don thought that Berle offered the best chance.

The last time I saw Mr. Berle, we talked of the matter. "When I first heard the story of Alger Hiss," he told me, "I was incredulous. But as I looked the evidence over, it was incontrovertible, and I arranged immediately for a talk with FDR.

"I never got more than half-way through, for the president, brimming with rage, refused to hear any more, so trustful was he of Hiss. He branded the tale as 'utter nonsense' and told me to take a flying jump in the lake for myself. (Note: I've softened the actual wording) and the next think I knew I had orders to go to South America."

But FDR wasn't the only one with complete faith in Hiss. There are still those who will tell you he was framed by FBI and that the famed Punkin Papers were planted, though happily these are now few.

[12.] Of American Jewish League against Communism.

Every tale has a moral and I suppose the lesson in this one is that it is unwise to be anti-Red prematurely. If you wish to be classified as a moderate—the ultimate in Newspeak accolade—wait till the Red evil is so evident that none can deny it.

Even then, though, after you've said your piece, it is wise to drop the matter and obliterate it from your mind—witness Hungary and Czechoslovakia. Who speaks of them now? You don't want to imperil the SALT talks, do you?

This is sound advice. If you doubt it, Rabbi Schultz, Don Levine and I have the scars to prove it.

The Author's Personal Thoughts

After Congregation, Beth Israel of Clarksdale, Mississippi, decided to sell the building housing its synagogue, most of the material of historic interest was taken and stored by the Institute of Southern Jewish Life of Jackson, Mississippi. There I found pictures of confirmation classes in the years when Rabbi Benjamin Schultz was working in Clarksdale. The problem was that the pictures had no names of the young people photographed. Stanley Kline—a member of our Vicksburg, Mississippi, congregation—suggested contacting a relative of his living in Clarksdale.

I went to Clarksdale to meet Aaron Kline, a man in his eighties blessed with an unusually sharp memory. He had no problem in recognizing all the faces in the pictures and telling stories about the families of the teenagers in the pictures.

Being in Clarksdale, it was natural for me to pay a visit to the final resting place of Rabbi Schultz and his wife, Charlotte. It was a pleasant afternoon in late May. The day was not hot but warm, and a light breeze made the visit enjoyable—as enjoyable as a visit to a cemetery can be.

In the quietness of this cemetery, many thoughts crossed my mind. In my lifetime, I have visited many Jewish cemeteries in different countries. I cannot describe the devastation I felt when I witnessed a desecrated Jewish cemetery. In their pathological aversion, the Jews' haters show their unwillingness to respect the right of the dead to an eternal rest. Any abandoned Jewish cemetery evokes thoughts of a past without a future, of achievements built on sand, and I never can forget that millions of Jewish people were never buried.

Here in Clarksdale, far away from the places where he was born and grew up in, far away from the place where his parents are buried, a Jew is interred. He was not a peddler or vagrant, nor was he a man passing by; he was a teacher of Israel. In this small Southern town, a rabbi is buried. To my best recollection, Rabbi Schultz is the only rabbi interred in the holy ground of this small Jewish cemetery. Rabbi Schultz came to this town from afar, scarred and bruised in the fight against evil and hunted mercilessly by some fellow Jews.

Hate and vengeance were rejected by this proud small Southern Jewish congregation that hired Rabbi Schultz to be its spiritual leader, and the people entrusted him with the Jewish education of their children. The Jewish congregation of Clarksdale offered Rabbi Schultz an abode, and he gave them his soul.

At my return to my home in Vicksburg, Mississippi, I inscribed Rabbi Benjamin Schultz's name in our congregational memorial book. At least once a year, his memory will be perpetuated and his life remembered. At the time, this was all I could do for the memory of late Rabbi Benjamin Schultz.

In Hebrew, there are many expressions said in praise of a dead person, and all can be said about Rabbi Benjamin Schultz. However, for Rabbi Schultz, the best fit would be *Leh L'Shalom*, "Go to peace." May God bestow on Rabbi Benjamin Schultz the eternal peace.

At the tenth anniversary of his rabbinical work in Clarksdale, Louise Moss Montgomery, a local poetess, wrote a poem in honor of Rabbi Schultz:

> We could say of Rabbi Schultz:
> Upon this rock of fortitude, our temple staunchly stands
> Because the One True God has put the priesthood in his hands
> This modern Levi humbly wears his treatments and his bands.

This is the way the people of Clarksdale, Jews and Christians alike, felt about Rabbi Schultz.

On Rabbi Schultz's tombstone, there is no epitaph. The above verses, if chiseled on the tombstone, would make a great epitaph.

The death of Rabbi Benjamin Schultz did not stop the controversies around his strong anti-Communism views. The difference is that now Schultz's writings and speeches can be found only in dusty newspapers of his day. Few people have the time to research the original sources. The lack of original sources many times leads to uninformed and nonobjective conclusions about Rabbi Schultz's work. I met Reform rabbis who were very anti-Schultz but never read the original articles that triggered the anti-Schultz campaign.

The anti-Schultz rhetoric started by accusing him of having the audacity to criticize Rabbi Stephen S. Wise. Shortly, this avenue of criticism was abandoned, and his critics found other reasons to disapprove of Rabbi Schultz's positions and views. In time, for many Reform rabbis and, unfortunately, some historians, the disapproval of Rabbi Schultz's work became a truism. Surprisingly, some teachers in academia adopted the same superficial approach attitude.

It was Rabbi Schultz who first pointed out and proved the intolerable situation of the Jews in the Soviet Union.

In combating Communism in the United States, Rabbi Schultz's message reached directly the American working middle-class and blue-collar people. These segments of the American population were not reached neither by the Jewish American Committee or the Anti-Defamation League.

Pioneering the study of Soviet Jewry and educating the American blue collar of the anti-Communist attitude and feelings of the American Jews are Rabbi Schultz's two historical achievements. Any professional, unbiased historian will give credit to Rabbi Schultz and at least for these two of his undeniable accomplishments.

My decision to write this small book was made with the sole intention of giving the modern reader partial access to original, archival material.

In the *Gates of Prayers the New Reform Prayer Book*, there is a parable attributed to Rabbi Chayim of Tanz. The text of this parable is as follows:

> A man was wandering lost in the forest for several days, finally encountered another. Brother, show me the way out of this forest! The man replied, "Brother, I too am lost. I can only tell you this: the ways I have tried lead nowhere, they have only led me astray. Take my hand and let us search for the way together."[13]

Like the man in the parable, Rabbi Benjamin Schultz pointed out that the Communist way does not solve the problems the Jewish people faced in the past twenty centuries. Without ideological arguments and without intellectual discussions, Rabbi Schultz in his speeches pointed out the facts. The criticism of Communism by Rabbi Schultz was direct and factual.

[13.] Stern, Chaim, *Gates of Prayer: The New Union Prayer Book* (New York: Central Conference of American Rabbis, 5735/1975), 349-350.

No fabrications of facts and no twisted information were used by Rabbi Schultz. His message was clear, direct, in plain English. Rabbi Schultz avoided pilpulistic arguments so much used by some Jewish intellectuals.[14] By this self-imposed standard, Rabbi Shultz gained the trust of the people who really were listening to his presentations.

Today, the anti-Schultz critics were partially successful in obliterating the contributions and achievements of Rabbi Schultz. However, sooner or later, history, will sort out the truth from the ideological hype.

"The principal responsibility of the thinking man is to make distinctions . . . Physics primers remind us that all of the progress of mankind to date has resulted from the making careful measurements." (William F. Buckley Jr.). History, like physics, is based on objective data and facts. Rabbi Benjamin Schultz's work, activities, and achievements deserve an objective assessment.

[14.] *Pilpulistic* (adjective) and *pilpulist* (noun) are rooted in the Hebrew word *pilpul* (a method of disputation that involves the development of careful and often excessively subtitle distinctions).

INDEX

A

Aaron, Henry, 9
Addes, George, 42
ADL. *See* Anti-Defamation League of B'nai B'rith
American Committee for Yugoslav Relief, 40
American Jewish Committee, 14, 39
American Jewish Labor Council, 59
American-Jewish League Against Communism, 22
American Jewry, 14, 53
American Legion and the Veterans of Foreign Wars, 15, 22, 50
American Peace Mobilization, 42
American way, 52
American Youth Congress, 33
American Youth for Democracy, 38
anti-Communism, 4, 71
Anti-Defamation League of B'nai B'rith, 15, 39
anti-Semitism, 13-15, 35, 37, 39, 41, 68
Aronson, Gregor, 69
Aronson, Philip, 61-62
Assn. of Catholic Trade Unionists, 40

B

Beth Israel Cemetery, Clarksdale, 21, 63
Beth Israel Temple. *See* Temple Beth Israel, Clarksdale
Bick, Rabbi Abraham, 38, 59
Biron, Phineas, 38
Bloch, Dr. Joshua, 38, 54, 59
Block, Harry, 40
Bolshevik, 26
Brainin, Joseph, 38
Bridges, Harry, 41-42
Britain, 37
Bronx, 44
Brooklyn, New York, 19, 27, 44-45, 47
Brooks, Lyle, 60
Browder, Earl, 33, 35
Brunswick, GA, 20, 22, 24, 28-29
Budenz, Louis F., 40
Bureau of Jewish Education, 37
Burgos, Mary, New York, 48

C

Carnegie Library, 11, 17
Catholic, 32, 35, 38-42, 46-47, 49, 59

Catholic Affairs Committee, 47
Catholic Church, 40-41
Catholic War Veterans, 41, 49
CCAR. *See* Central Conference of American Rabbis
Center of Jewish History, 17
Central Conference of American Rabbis, 20, 27, 58, 72
Chapman, Abraham, 41
Chapman, Dr. Emmanuel, 40-42
churches. *See various churches*
Chworowsky, Rev. Karl, 36
CIO. *See* Jewish People's Fraternal Order
Clarksdale, MS, 9, 11, 17, 20, 22-25, 27-29, 62-64, 68, 70-71
Clarksdale Press Register (newspaper), 21, 23, 63
Clarksdale Rotary Club, 22
Coahoma County Ministerial Association, 22, 29
Cohn, Roy M., 26
Commercial Appeal, The, Memphis, TN, 23, 68
commies, 32, 39, 41, 44, 46
Committee of Catholics for Human Rights, 40
Committee on Un-American Activities, 25
Communism, 4, 13-15, 20, 22-28, 32, 35, 40-42, 45-47, 49, 51-54, 60, 63, 65, 69, 71-72
Communist International Order. *See* Jewish People's Fraternal Order
Congress, 33
congressional record, 28
Congress on Civil Rights, 40
Connelly, Philip M., 42

Council for Pan American Democracy, 40
Cronbach, Rabbi and Prof. Abraham, 39, 59

D

Daily Worker (newspaper), 33, 35, 38, 40-42
Daily Yiddish Forward (newspaper), 25, 29, 39
Danziger, Rabbi Harry, 21
Darr, Rev. John (Methodist), 33-34, 59
Delta Rhe (prize), 58
Detroit, 41
Dixie. See Wilkie, Curtis
Dress and Waistmakers Union, 43
Dubinsky, David, 37
Dulles, John Foster, 34

E

Edlin, William, 38
Eisler, Gerhart, 33, 59
Eisler, Hilda, 59
Elkind, Charlotte. *See* Schultz, Charlotte Elkind
Emanu-El, Temple. *See* Temple Emanu-El, Yonkers
Episcopal Church League for Industrial Democracy, 33

F

fascism, 33, 39, 58
Federal Council of Churches of Christ, 34
fellow-travelers, 24, 29, 40, 69

Fitzgerald, Albert P., 40
Flatbush Unitarian Church, 36
Fogel, Y., 25
Fordham University, 41
Forward. See *Daily Yiddish Forward*
Foster, William Z., 35-36
Freiheit (Communist Yiddish newspaper), 38-39, 41, 56
Fritchman, Dr. Stephen H., 34
fronts, 32, 36, 40-41, 57
Fuchs, Walter T., Yonkers, New York, 52

G

Gailmor, William, 38
Gallagher, Leo, 41
Germany, 15, 34, 42
Gold, Ben, 37-38
Goldberg, B. Z., 38
Golditch, Leonard, 37-38
Gottesman, George, Mrs. (sister), 22, 25, 29
Granison, Abram M. (rabbi), 50
Gray, Horace M., Yonkers, New York, 51
Greece, 33

H

Harlem, 35
Harry Bridges Defense Committee, 41
Hebrew, 11, 15, 22, 37, 39, 56-57, 59-60, 66, 71, 73
Hebrew Union Collage, Cincinnati, OH, 39
Hebrew Union Collage-Jewish Institute of Religion, 11, 22

Herald Statesman, The (newspaper), 28, 51-53, 61, 65
Hitler, 33, 57, 59
Holy Trinity Church, Brooklyn, 33
Hollywood, 41
Hollywood Independent Citizens Committee of Arts, Sciences and Professions, 41
Hollywood Writers Mobilization, 41
Holmes, Rev. John Haynes, 36
Hunter College, 41

I

Ickes, Harold L., 34
Ihda, Fred, Jr., New Jersey, 46
Independent Citizens Committee of Arts, Sciences and Professions, Hollywood, 41
International Ladies Garment Workers Union, 37
Isaacson, Abe, 17, 62-63

J

Jewish, 7, 11, 14-15, 17, 19-20, 22-24, 26-29, 32, 35-39, 45-46, 50, 53-54, 56-59, 63-64, 68-73
Jewish Community Relations Advisory Council, 35, 38
Jewish Council to Aid Russian Rehabilitation, 37
Jewish Council to Aid the Rehabilitation of Russia, 59
Jewish Day (newspaper), 38
Jewish Institute of Religion, 11, 19-20, 27, 29, 50
Jewish Labor Committee, 39
Jewish Labor Council, 59

Jewish National Post (newspaper), 29
Jewish People's Fraternal Order, 26, 36-38, 59
Jews, 4, 14-15, 17, 24, 27, 29, 33, 35-40, 42, 45-47, 54, 56-58, 67-72
JPFO. *See* Jewish People's Fraternal Order

K

Kahn, Albert E., 36, 38
Kaplan, Morris, 24
Kennedy, Matthew F., New York, 47
Kernan, Rev. William C., 36
Kincade, Kat, 9
King, Martin Luther, Jr., 9
Kline, Aaron, 70
Kline, Stanley, 70
Knights of Columbus, 35, 47
Kossman, Paul, 17
Kreindler, Charles, 26

L

Labor Council, 39, 59
Lavery, Emmet, 41-42
League of American Writers, 40
LeCompte, Viva, New York, 49
Lee, V., New York, 46
Lenin, 33
Leslie, Kenneth, 35
Library of Congress, 11, 34
Los Angeles, 37, 41, 63, 68
Los Angeles Jewish Community Council, 37
Lowell, James Russell, 23

M

Magdovitz, Lawrence M., 17, 64
Mahr, Mrs. Louis, 22, 25, 29
Margolis. *See* Gailmor, William
Marshal Plan, 34
Marx, Karl, 35, 38
Marxism, 33, 38, 41
May Day, 33
McCarthy, Senator Joseph R., 25, 64
McMichael, Rev. Jack, 33-34
McNeil Funeral Home, 21
Mc. Nelty, Rebecca V., New York, 44
Melish, Rev. William Howard, 33-34
Memphis, 21-22, 68
Methodist, 33, 59
Methodist Bishop Lewis O. Hartman, Boston, 33
Methodist Federation for Social Service, 33
Miakoff, Nathaniel M., New York, 43
Mobilization for Democracy, 41
Morford, Rev. Richard (Presbyterian), 33-34
Morning Freiheit (newspaper), 38
Moscow, 42, 69

N

National Committee to Combat Anti-Semitism, 41
National Conference of Christians and Jews, 24, 29
National Council for American-Soviet Friendship, 33
National Jewish Post (newspaper), 29, 32, 36, 58
Nazi, 36, 57, 69
Nelson, Louis, 26

Nevins, Bessie L., Yonkers, New York, 51
New Leader, The (newspaper), 58
New Masses, 35
New York Board of Rabbis, 23-24, 28
New York Public Library Jewish Division, 38
New York Times, 24
New York University, 61
New York World-Telegram. See *World-Telegram* (newspaper)
Niebuhr, Dr. Reinhold, 36
non-Communist, 36
Notre Dame University, 41
Novick, P., 38

O

O'Keefe, Kinchen H., 17
Orthodox Congregation Oheb Zedek, East Pittsburgh, PA, 37

P

Palestine, 36, 39
Paul Harris Fellowship, 29
Peoples Institute for Applied Religion, 32
Petrusello, G., 47
Pius XII (pope), 40, 42
Poland, 42, 69
Presbyterian, 32-33
Presbyterian Peoples Institute for Applied Religion, 32
pro-Communist, 34, 37-38
Protestant, 32, 34-39, 46, 57, 59
Protestant, The (magazine), 35, 37-38
Pulitzer Prize, 57-58

Q

Quill, Michael J., 40, 42

R

rabbi, 7, 9, 13-15, 17, 19-29, 32, 36, 38-39, 42-73
Red Channels, 25
"Red Crocodiles Tears Ensnare Some Rabbis," 36, 57
"Red Fronts Find Dupes in Protestant Pulpits," 32, 57
"Reds Use Prominent Catholics as Bait to Lure Masses," 39, 57
Religious Education Committee, 58
Reporter, Hollywood, 29, 41
Richardson, Rev. Ben, 35
Rochester (university), NY, 58
Roosevelt (president), 33, 42, 68
Rotary, 20, 22-23, 25, 28-29, 35, 63
Rotary Club, 20, 22, 29, 35, 63
Rotary International. See Rotary
Rusher, William A., 23
Russia, 33-34, 36-37, 39, 42, 59, 68-69
Russian Rehabilitation Council, 38
Ryskind, Morrie, 68

S

Sandler, Gedaliah, 36
Schappes, Morris U., 38, 56
Schiller, Rivka, 25
School for Jewish Studies, 38-39
Schultz, Benjamin (rabbi), 9, 13-15, 17, 19, 21-29, 32, 36, 39, 43-52, 56, 58-73
Schultz, Charlotte Elkind, 17, 19, 22, 25, 27, 29, 61-62, 64, 70

Schultz, Clement, 22, 25, 29
Schultz, Morris, 25, 29
Schultz, Robert, 22, 25, 29
Screen Writers Guild, 41
Scripps-Howard (newspapers), 22, 50
Seldes, George, 34
sharecropper preachers, 35
Shipler, Rev. Guy Emery, 34
Siberia, 37, 69
Sound View Foundation Inc., 35
Soviet-American Friendship Council, 34
Soviet Jewry, 13-15, 72
Soviet Jews, 14-15
Soviet Union, 13-15, 17, 42, 72
Spofford, Rev. William B., 33-35
Stalin, 35-36, 39-40, 42
State Committee of the Communist Party, 32
Stepinac (archbishop), 42

T

Telegano, Ralph de, 48
Temple Ahavath Shalom, Brooklyn, NY, 27
Temple Beth Israel, Clarksdale, 20-22, 24, 27-29
Temple Beth Tefilloh, Brunswick, GA, 20, 28
Temple Emanu-El, Yonkers, 19-20, 23-24, 28, 50, 52, 61, 65
Temple Israel, Memphis, 21
Tenney, Jack B. (state senator of California), 41
Timms, Josephine, 42
Tito, 34
Toronto, Canada, 27
Transport Workers Union, 40
Truman doctrine, 34

U

Union of American Hebrew Congregations, 59
Unitarian Christian Register, 34
United Auto Workers, 42
United Christian Council for Democracy, 33
United Electrical, Radio and Machine Workers, 40
United Jewish Appeal, 37

V

Vatican, 42

W

Walsh, J. Raymond, 40, 42
Ward, Dr. Harry F. (Methodist), 33
Weekly Digest of the Jewish Press, 29
Westchester, NY, 20, 32, 36, 39, 61
White, Linda, 17
White, Rev. Eliot, 32
White House, 33-34
Wilkie, Curtis, 9
Williams, Rev. Claude, 32, 34, 38
Wise, Rabbi Stephen S., 29, 36, 53-54, 59, 72
Witness, The, 33-34
Woltman (columnist), 44-45, 56-58
Wood, Lee B., 57
World-Telegram (newspaper), 23-24, 28, 32, 36, 39, 43-51, 56-59
Writers Congress, pro-Soviet, 41

Y

Yiddish, 17
Yonkers, 17, 20, 22-25, 27-29, 50-51, 58-62, 65, 67-68
Young Communist League, 38
Youth for Democracy. *See* American Youth for Democracy
Yugoslavia, 34

Z

Zimmerman, Charles, 37
Zionism, 37
Zionist(s), 20, 32, 36-39

CPSIA information can be obtained at www.ICGtesting.com
Printed in the USA
LVOW070243070512
280610LV00002B/2/P